PRIMARY
PARTNERS

A- Z Activities
to Make Learning Fun

for Ages 8-11
Doctrine and Covenants/Church History

46 Learning Activities

Simple Supplies Needed ◘ Matching Thought Treats

46 Scripture Challenge Cards with Reward Glue-on Stickers

**Use for Primary Lessons, Family Home Evening,
and Daily Devotionals to Reinforce Gospel Topics**

You'll Find: A-Z Topics to Match Primary Lessons

Apostasy   Articles of Faith   Baptism for the Dead   Bishops

Book of Mormon   Celestial Kingdom   Commandments   Faith

First Vision   Forgiveness   Gifts of the Spirit   Gospel Fulness

Gratitude   Holy Ghost   Hymns   Law of Consecration

Love and Unity   Missionary   Obedience   Ordinances Restored

Pioneer Spirit   Prayer   Prepare   Priesthood Blessings/Keys

Prophets   Restoration   Revelation   Sabbath Day   Sacrifice

Scriptures   Second Coming   Service   Temple Marriage   Temples

Testimony   Tithing   Trials   Valiant   Word of Wisdom

97 98 99 00 01 02   10 9 8 7 6 5 4 3 2 1

Primary Partners: Doctrine and Covenants/Church History—Ages 8–11

Covenant Communications, Inc.
ISBN 1-57734-065-5

INTRODUCTION
PRIMARY PARTNERS:
A-Z Activities to Make Learning Fun
Doctrine and Covenants/Church History
for Primary 5* Ages 8-11

Primary teachers and parents, you'll enjoy using the PRIMARY PARTNERS activities to supplement your Primary lessons, enhance your family home evenings, and help children learn gospel principles in fun, challenging ways. Children love these easy, fun-to-create visuals. Patterns for each project are actual size, ready to Copy-n-Create in minutes to make learning fun.

How to Use This Book

1. **Preview A-Z Table of Contents** for visuals to match your gospel subject.

2. **Use the Lesson Cross Reference Index** on page iv to match lessons #1-46 in the manual*.

3. **Copy Patterns Ahead.** You'll save time and avoid last minute preparation.

4. **Shop Ahead For Simple Supplies.** Each activity requires a few basic items: Copies of patterns, scissors, crayons, tape, glue, zip-close plastic bags, paper punch, yarn or ribbon, metal brads, and pencils.

5. **Organize Activities** A-Z (for family home evening use), or #1-46 (for Primary lessons). Copy instructions to include with the pattern copies and supplies.

6. **Activity Journal:** Provide each child with a 3-ring binder or folder to store classroom creations. Encourage children to display activities in their room for a few weeks before placing them in their notebook. Include in notebooks the "I'm Trying to Be Like Jesus" cover page with the child's picture next to Jesus. Children can fill in their personal goals and information.

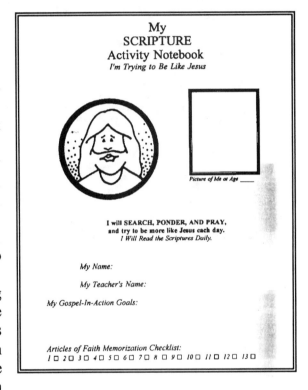

My
SCRIPTURE
Activity Notebook
I'm Trying to Be Like Jesus

Picture of Me at Age ____

I will SEARCH, PONDER, AND PRAY,
and try to be more like Jesus each day.
I Will Read the Scriptures Daily.

My Name:

My Teacher's Name:

My Gospel-In-Action Goals:

Articles of Faith Memorization Checklist:
1☐ 2☐ 3☐ 4☐ 5☐ 6☐ 7☐ 8 ☐ 9☐ 10☐ 11☐ 12☐ 13☐

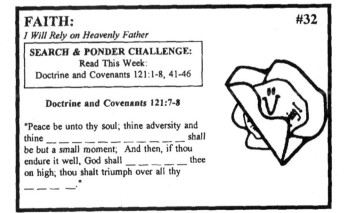

FAITH: #32
I Will Rely on Heavenly Father

SEARCH & PONDER CHALLENGE:
Read This Week:
Doctrine and Covenants 121:1-8, 41-46

Doctrine and Covenants 121:7-8

"Peace be unto thy soul; thine adversity and thine _ _ _ _ _ _ _ _ _ _ _ shall be but a small moment; And then, if thou endure it well, God shall _ _ _ _ _ thee on high; thou shalt triumph over all thy _ _ _ _ _."

7. **Scripture Challenge Cards:** You'll find Scripture Challenge Cards in numerical order #1-46 to match lessons #1-46*. ♥ Challenge Scripture Reading. Assign a SCRIPTURE CHALLENGE CARD each week (see patterns on pages 90-113). Children can read the scriptures assigned and fill in the blanks on the featured scripture. ♥ Reward for Scripture Reading. As children bring the completed card the next week, reward them with a large glue-on sticker to match the image on the card. This larger sticker shows the children that their testimony grows as they read the scriptures. ♥ Help Children Organize Cards. Option #1: Create a book by punching holes in card tabs and lace or ring them together. See book cover label on page 90. Option #2: Store cards in a zip-close plastic bag (cutting left tab off). Place the label in front of cards.

*Primary 5 manual is published by The Church of Jesus Christ of Latter-day Saints, Salt Lake City, Utah.

My
SCRIPTURE
Activity Notebook
I'm Trying to Be Like Jesus

Picture of Me at Age _____

I will SEARCH, PONDER, AND PRAY,
and try to be more like Jesus each day.
I Will Read the Scriptures Daily.

My Name:

My Teacher's Name:

My Gospel-In-Action Goals:

Articles of Faith Memorization Checklist:
1 ☐ *2* ☐ *3* ☐ *4* ☐ *5* ☐ *6* ☐ *7* ☐ *8* ☐ *9* ☐ *10* ☐ *11* ☐ *12* ☐ *13* ☐

LESSON CROSS REFERENCE INDEX to Primary Doctrine and Covenants/Church History manual*

*Primary 5 manual is published by The Church of Jesus Christ of Latter-day Saints, Salt Lake City, Utah.

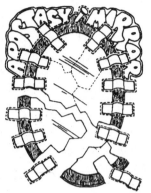

APOSTASY: Jesus Christ's Church Is Restored (apostasy mirror) 1-3

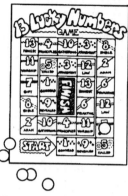

ARTICLES OF FAITH Strengthen My Testimony (key word maze) 4-5

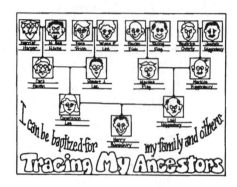

BAPTISM FOR DEAD: I Can Be Baptized for Others (pedigree) . . 4, 6-7

BISHOPS: I Will Support My Church Leaders (Bishop Bingo) 8-12

BOOK OF MORMON: I Will Bear My Testimony (doorknob hanger) . . . 13-15

BOOK OF MORMON: I'm Grateful (typesetting poster) 13, 16-17

CELESTIAL: I Can Live with Heavenly Father (connected kingdoms) 18-20

COMMANDMENTS: I Will Be Blessed as I Obey (Promise Puzzle) 21-22

FAITH: Faith in Christ Helps Me (Jesus light-switch cover) 21, 23

FAITH: I Will Rely on Heavenly Father (bite-size memorize) 24-25

FIRST VISION: Joseph Saw Heavenly Father and Jesus (bookmark) 24, 26

FORGIVENESS: I Will Forgive Others (bite-size memorize) 27-28

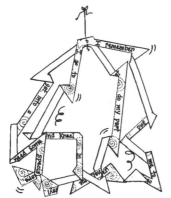

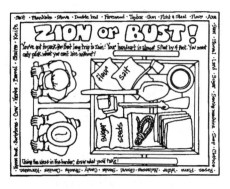

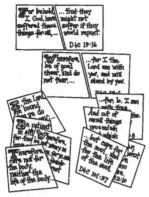

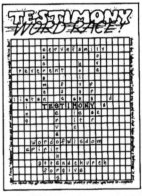

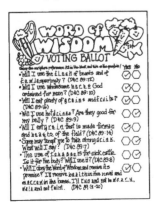
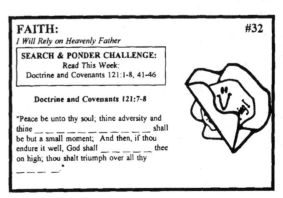

APOSTASY: Jesus Christ's Church Is Restored

(apostasy mirror puzzle teaching tool)

See lesson #2 in Primary 5 manual*.

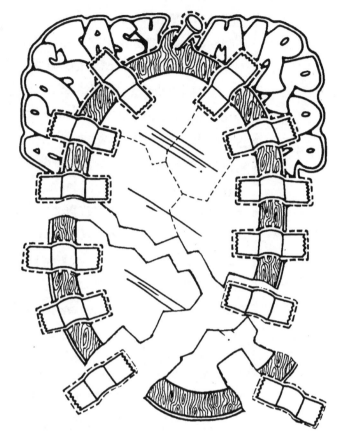

YOU'LL NEED: Copy of Apostasy Mirror bag label and Apostasy Mirror puzzle patterns (pages 2-3) and SCRIPTURE CHALLENGE CARD (page 91) on colored cardstock paper, and a zip-close plastic bag for each child, scissors, and crayons

ACTIVITY: Create a teaching tool children can show their families about the apostasy and restoration of the Church of Jesus Christ.
1. Color and cut out apostasy mirror puzzle pieces and bag label.
2. Read label to children and show puzzle.
3. Place label inside plastic bag with puzzle pieces for children to teach their family and friends.

SCRIPTURE CHALLENGE CARD: Assign each child a new card and reward them with a glue-on sticker for the card completed.

THOUGHT TREAT: Apostasy Cookie Crumble. Show a sandwich type cookie filled with frosting that you can take apart (i.e., Oreo® cookie). Talk about the apostasy, saying Option #1 or Option #2 as follows.

OPTION #1:
Jesus organized the Church of Jesus Christ when he was on the earth. After he and his 12 apostles died, the truth crumbled (separate cookie into two parts and crumble one cookie half). Christ's teachings broke away into many different beliefs. Then Joseph Smith prayed to find the true church. Because he asked Heavenly Father for the truth, The Church of Jesus Christ of Latter-day Saints was restored (take a good half of another cookie and place it on top of the frosting to make a complete sandwich cookie).

OPTION #2:
The Bible is <u>one</u> testament of Jesus Christ (show one side of cookie), and the Book of Mormon is <u>another</u> testament of Jesus Christ (show other side of cookie). We can study the Bible and Book of Mormon and pray to know of the truth they hold. Our prayers help us gain a firm testimony that helps us keep the commandments, like the frosting that holds these two cookies together. As we search, ponder, and pray about these scriptures, we can gain a firm testimony that the Church of Jesus Christ was restored in these latter days. (Review the 8th Article of Faith.)

PRIMARY PARTNERS Doctrine and Covenants/Church History Ages 8-11

PATTERN: APOSTASY (apostasy mirror sack label to store puzzle)   See lesson #2 in Primary 5 manual*.

The Apostasy Mirror

This mirror represents the Church of Jesus Christ. The mirror represents the church itself, with Christ at the top as the nail and each of the apostles as a piece of tape. When Christ died the apostles held up the mirror and took care of the affairs of the Church. When the apostles were killed, the mirror fell and broke, thus resulting in the apostasy. But people still saw good in the mirror and took pieces and built around them resulting in the many varied churches we have today. This exemplifies the reason we needed a <u>restoration</u> and not just a reformation....because a mirror that has been broken cannot be repaired--it must be replaced.

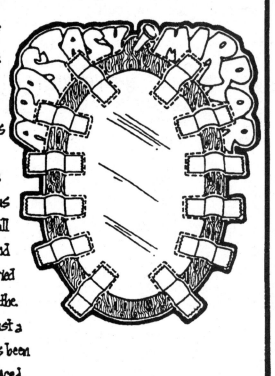

The Apostasy Mirror

This mirror represents the Church of Jesus Christ. The mirror represents the church itself, with Christ at the top as the nail and each of the apostles as a piece of tape. When Christ died the apostles held up the mirror and took care of the affairs of the Church. When the apostles were killed, the mirror fell and broke, thus resulting in the apostasy. But people still saw good in the mirror and took pieces and built around them resulting in the many varied churches we have today. This exemplifies the reason we needed a <u>restoration</u> and not just a reformation....because a mirror that has been broken cannot be repaired--it must be replaced.

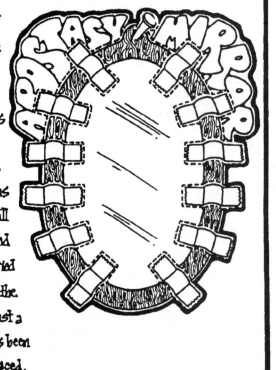

*Primary 5 manual is published by The Church of Jesus Christ of Latter-day Saints, Salt Lake City, Utah.

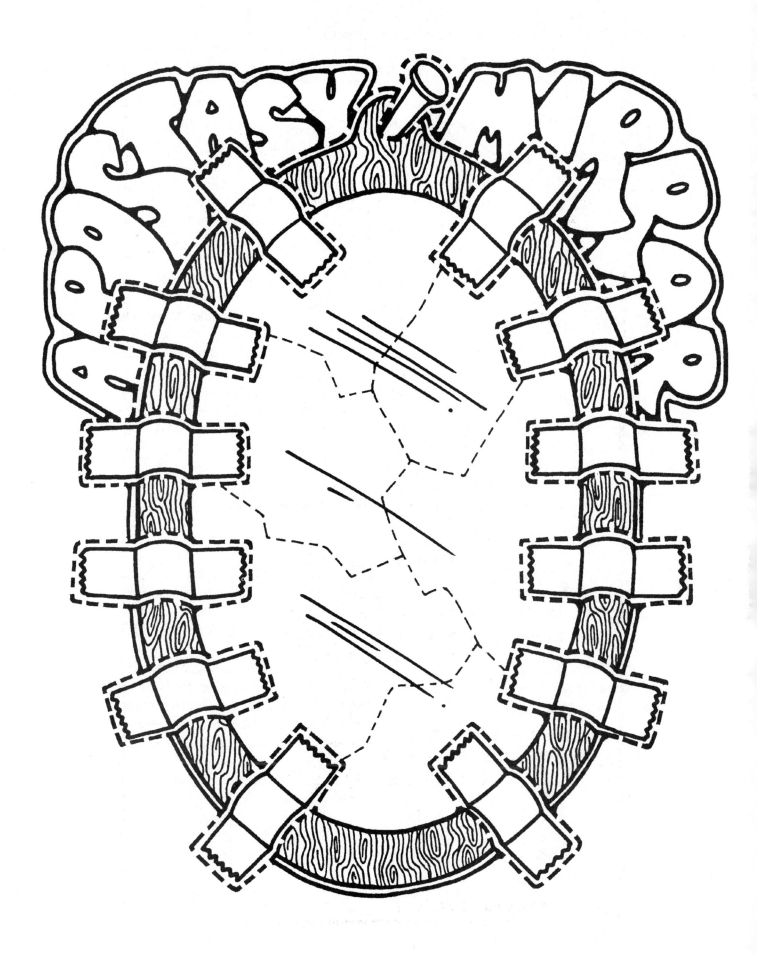

ARTICLES OF FAITH Strengthen My Testimony

(Articles of Faith Lucky Numbers Game)

See lesson #36 in Primary 5 manual*.

YOU'LL NEED: Copy of Articles of Faith Lucky Numbers Game board pattern (page 5), SCRIPTURE CHALLENGE CARD (page 108) on colored cardstock paper for each child, scissors, pencils, crayons, two different coins (markers), and a die (or instead of using a die, copy and cut out MOVE 1-5 markers on page 50)

ACTIVITY: Play the Articles of Faith Lucky Numbers Game to learn the key words and learn the Articles of Faith.
Color and cut out game board.

TO PLAY: (1) Divide into two teams. (2) Place a marker for each team at START. First team rolls the die or chooses a MOVE 1-5 marker (page 50) and places a coin or marker on number rolled or drawn. (3) When team lands on number, look at the Articles of Faith key word. (4) If person playing can say the Article of Faith, he earns 10 points for their team. (5) The first team to get to FINISH wins 100 points.

*SCRIPTURE CHALLENGE**

THOUGHT TREAT: Lucky 13 Cookies. Write numbers 1, 2, 3, 4, 5, 6, 7, 8, 9, 10, 11, 12, and 13 on 13 different sugar cookies using frosting in a tube. Have the child who eats the numbered cookie recite the Article of Faith belonging to that number.

BAPTISM FOR THE DEAD: I Can Be Baptized for Others

(Tracing My Ancestors—art fun)

See lesson #34 in Primary 5 manual*.

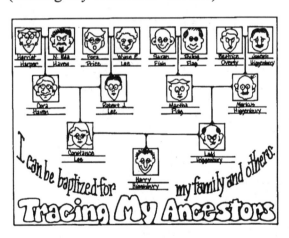

YOU'LL NEED: Copy of poster and hair and facial features patterns (pages 6-7) on lightweight paper, and SCRIPTURE CHALLENGE CARD (page 107) on colored cardstock paper for each child, pencils, and crayons

ACTIVITY: Create a fun pedigree chart children can trace their ancestors three generations. Tell children that families can be linked together forever as each child is sealed to his or her parents. We can search family history records to see if baptisms and family sealings have been done. If not, we can submit names to the temple for this important work.

(1) Hold the Tracing My Ancestors pedigree chart to the window with hair and facial features behind chart. With light shining through, create each ancestor by tracing hair and facial features into each box (starting with your own family).

(2) Write in the names of each ancestor to complete the family group chart.

*SCRIPTURE CHALLENGE**

THOUGHT TREAT: Graham Crackers and Milk. Baptize the graham cracker by immersion in the milk and think of your ancestors.

**SCRIPTURE CHALLENGE: Assign each child a new card and reward them with a glue-on sticker for the card completed.

Tracing My Ancestors

I can be baptized for my family and others.

PATTERN: BAPTISM FOR THE DEAD (Tracing My Ancestors—art fun)   See lesson #34 in Primary 5 manual*.

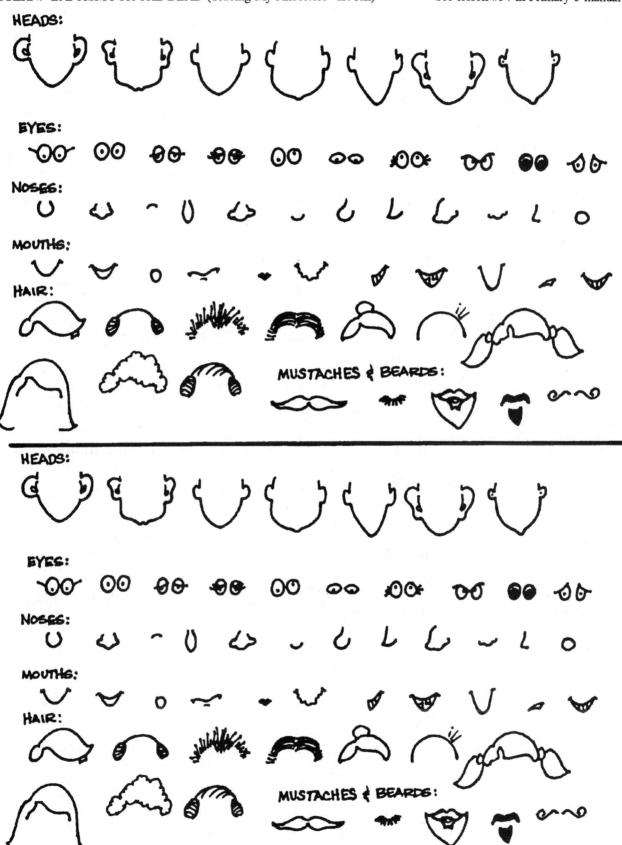

*Primary 5 manual is published by The Church of Jesus Christ of Latter-day Saints, Salt Lake City, Utah.

7

BISHOPS: I Will Support My Church Leaders

(Bishop Bingo)

See lesson #17 in Primary 5 manual*.

YOU'LL NEED: Copy of clue sheet (below) and Bishop Bingo card patterns (pages 9-11), SCRIPTURE CHALLENGE CARD (page 99) on colored cardstock paper, and 25 pieces of candy, beans, macaroni, coins, or cut up squares of paper for markers for each child, scissors, and crayons

ACTIVITY: Play Bishop Bingo to help children learn the various things a bishop or his counselors might do to guide us.

AHEAD OF TIME: Copy and cut out clue sheet (below) and place in a hat or box to draw from. Cut out a bingo card for each child.

TO PLAY: (1) Give each child a different card if playing with eight children. More than eight children can play if they know that another child may have a card that matches the one they have. (2) Give each child 10 or more markers (candy, beans, etc.). (3) Children can take turns drawing clues from a hat or box and calling the bingo square. (4) When player's bingo card picture matches the clue, player can cover the square with a marker. (5) Play until winner has a row of five marked squares (left, right, or diagonal) and announces "Bishop Bingo!"

SCRIPTURE CHALLENGE CARD: Assign each child a new card and reward them with a glue-on sticker for the card completed.

Wants you to Choose the Right (CTR)	Temple interview	Supervises Leaders
Receives revelation	Has a testimony	Prays for ward
Interview for baptism	Can be a friend	Fasts for the ward
Shakes your hand	Give a member a calling	Gives a blessing
Helps members repent	Visits the sick	Can help with problems
Can be a good example	Conducts meetings	Counsels a member
Greets with a smile	Accepts your tithing	Loves the ward
Helps a needy family	Visits a ward member	Teaches the gospel

THOUGHT TREAT: Sweet Bishop Cookie. Give children a sugar cookie and talk about the sweet blessings the bishop brings to your ward or branch family. Also say, "The sweet taste of this cookie makes us feel happy. The sweet testimony that the bishop and his counselors share gives us a happy, peaceful feeling."

*Primary 5 manual is published by The Church of Jesus Christ of Latter-day Saints, Salt Lake City, Utah.

BISHOP BINGO

Card 2

Visits the sick	Counsels a member	Accept your tithing	Gives a member a calling	Interview for baptism
Supervises leaders	Gives a blessing	Helps a needy family	Can be a good example	Greets with a smile
Helps members repent	Can be a friend	FREE!	Temple Interview	Has a testimony
Conducts meetings	Fasts for the Ward	Teaches the gospel	Visits a Ward member	Receives revelation
Prays for the Ward	Can help with problems	Loves the Ward	Shakes your hand	Wants you to CTR

BISHOP BINGO

Card 1

Wants you to CTR	Temple Interview	Receives revelation	Has a testimony	Prays for the Ward
Interview for baptism	Supervises leaders	Can be a friend	Fasts for the Ward	Shakes your hand
Gives a member a calling	Gives a blessing	FREE!	Helps members repent	Visits the sick
Can help with problems	Can be a good example	Conducts meetings	Counsels a member	Greets with a smile
Accepts your tithing	Loves the Ward	Helps a needy family	Visits a Ward member	Teaches the gospel

BISHOP BINGO

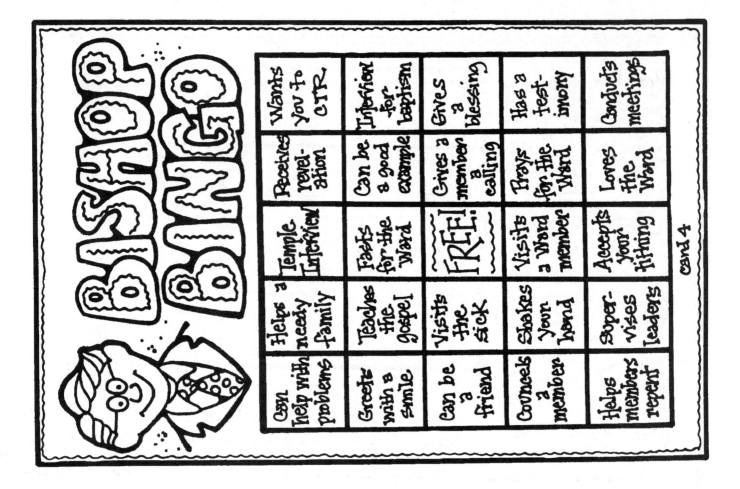

Wants you to CTR	Received revelation	Temple Interview	Helps a needy family	Can help with problems
Interview for baptism	Can be a good example	Fasts for the Ward	Teaches the gospel	Greets with a smile
Gives a blessing	Gives a member a calling	FREE!	Visits the sick	Can be a friend
Has a testimony	Prays for the Ward	Visits a Ward member	Shakes your hand	Counsels a member
Conducts meetings	Loves the Ward	Accepts your tithing	Supervises leaders	Helps members repent

card 4

BISHOP BINGO

Greets with a smile	Supervises leaders	Teaches the gospel	Receives revelation	Wants you to CTR
Accepts your tithing	Helps a needy family	Shakes your hand	Has a testimony	Can be a friend
Prays for the Ward	Conducts meetings	FREE!	Temple Interview	Loves the Ward
Fasts for the Ward	Gives a blessing	Help members repent	Can be a good example	Can help with problems
Gives a member a calling	Counsels a member	Visits the sick	Interview for baptism	Visits a Ward member

card 5

BISHOP BINGO

Receives revelation	Wants you to CTR	Helps members repent	Can help with problems	Can be a good example
Interview for baptism	Temple Interview	Fasts for the Ward	Accepts your tithing	Greets with a smile
Helps a needy family	Gives a member a calling	FREE!	Teaches the gospel	Visits the sick
Has a testimony	Shakes your hand	Can be a friend	Prays for the Ward	Conducts meetings
Visits a ward member	Loves the Ward	Gives a blessing	Counsels a member	Supervises leaders

card 6

BISHOP BINGO

Visits the sick	Has a testimony	Receives revelation	Accepts your tithing	Wants you to CTR
Conducts meetings	Helps a needy family	Helps members repent	Can help with problems	Loves the Ward
Gives a member a calling	Fasts for the Ward	FREE!	Can be a good example	Interview for baptism
Teaches the gospel	Shake your hand	Temple Interview	Supervises leaders	Visits a ward member
Counsels a member	Gives a blessing	Prays for the Ward	Can be a friend	Greets with a smile

card 5

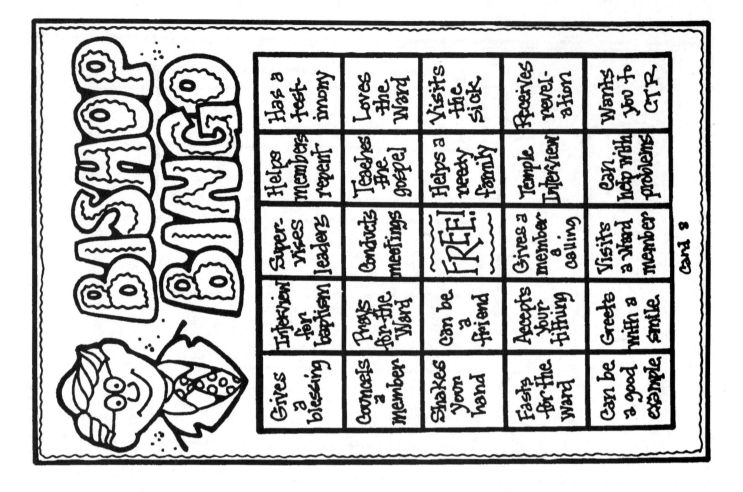

BISHOP BINGO

Has a testimony	Helps members repent	Supervises leaders	Interview for baptism	Gives a blessing
Loves the Ward	Teaches the gospel	Conducts meetings	Prays for the Ward	Counsels a member
Visits the sick	Helps a needy family	FREE!	Can be a friend	Shakes your hand
Receives revelation	Temple Interview	Gives a member a calling	Accepts your tithing	Fasts for the Ward
Wants you to CTR	Can help with problems	Visits a ward member	Greets with a smile	Can be a good example

Card 8

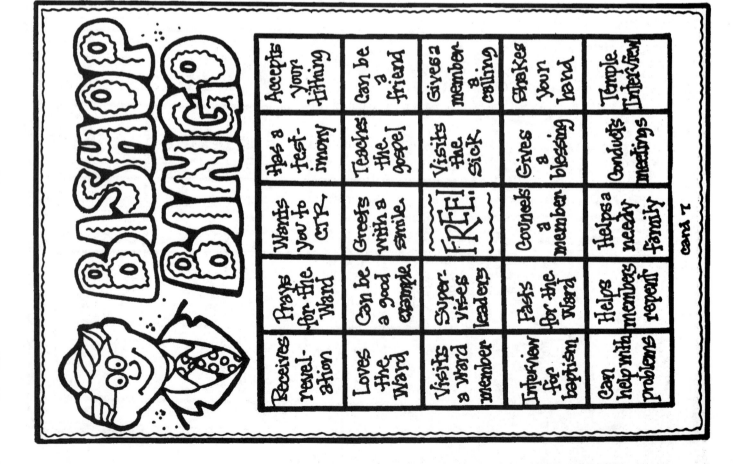

BISHOP BINGO

Accepts your tithing	Has a testimony	Wants you to CTR	Prays for the Ward	Receives revelation
Can be a friend	Teaches the gospel	Greets with a smile	Can be a good example	Loves the Ward
Gives a member a calling	Visits the sick	FREE!	Supervises leaders	Visits a ward member
Shakes your hand	Gives a blessing	Counsels a member	Fasts for the Ward	Interview for baptism
Temple Interview	Conducts meetings	Helps a needy family	Helps members repent	Can help with problems

Card 7

BOOK OF MORMON: I Will Bear My Testimony of Truth

(testimony bear slide show/doorknob hanger)

See lesson #9 in Primary 5 manual*.

YOU'LL NEED: Copy of testimony bear slide show pattern (pages 14-15) and SCRIPTURE CHALLENGE CARD (page 95) on colored cardstock paper for each child, scissors, glue, and crayons

ACTIVITY: Children can learn ways to be a witness of the Book of Mormon and its teachings. They can learn how to bear their testimony of the gospel of Jesus Christ.
(1) Color and cut out bear, bow, and doorknob hanger (slide show). (2) Boys glue bow tie on bear and girls glue bow on head. (3) Glue part A and B together where shown. (4) Cut a slit in the top and bottom on square on bear's tummy.
(5) Slide doorknob hanger (slide show wordstrips) down into bear to pull up and down. (6) Fold bottom flap of wordstrip to prevent slipping. (7) Children can take home and hang on their door.

*SCRIPTURE CHALLENGE***

THOUGHT TREAT: Testimony Bear Treats. Make a bear using a bear mold and Rice Krispies® recipe (on box of Kellogg's® cereal). Or, make bear using bread dough and bake. Or, give cinnamon candy bears to children.
Ask children to bear their testimony in class and then eat the bear.

BOOK OF MORMON PUBLICATION: I'm Grateful to Have It

(typesetting poster)

See lesson #10 in Primary 5 manual*.

YOU'LL NEED: Copy of typesetting poster and letter patterns (pages 16-17) and SCRIPTURE CHALLENGE CARD (page 95) on colored cardstock paper for each child, scissors, glue, and crayons

ACTIVITY: Remind children that the Book of Mormon was first published by setting the metal type by hand. It was a lot of work, but it was worth the effort to make the Book of Mormon available to people everywhere. Children can set type by placing the letters to read: "THE BOOK OF MORMON: ANOTHER TESTAMENT OF JESUS CHRIST" in the spaces provided on the poster. *TYPESET POSTER:* Have children cut out letters needed to "set the type," placing spaces where necessary, and color the poster.

*SCRIPTURE CHALLENGE***

THOUGHT TREAT: ABC Pancakes. Cook pancakes on a hot skillet in the shape of A, B, and C. Colorful Option: Color batter three different colors, i.e., pink to make the A's, blue to make the B's, and yellow to make the C's.

**SCRIPTURE CHALLENGE: Assign each child a new card and reward them with a glue-on sticker for the card. completed.

*Primary 5 manual is published by The Church of Jesus Christ of Latter-day Saints, Salt Lake City, Utah.

13

PATTERN: BOOK OF MORMON (testimony slide show)

See lesson #9 in Primary 5 manual*.

*Bow can be a bowtie for the boys and a hair bow for the girls!

I will "bear" my testimony of truth.

*Primary 5 manual is published by The Church of Jesus Christ of Latter-day Saints, Salt Lake City, Utah.

Part A

Part B

Glue to part A

Joseph Smith translated the Book of Mormon through God's power.

The True Priesthood was restored.

We have a living Prophet today.

Jesus Christ lives and loves me.

The Holy Ghost speaks truth to my heart.

Fold back

The Book of Mormon is true.

Joseph Smith is God's chosen prophet.

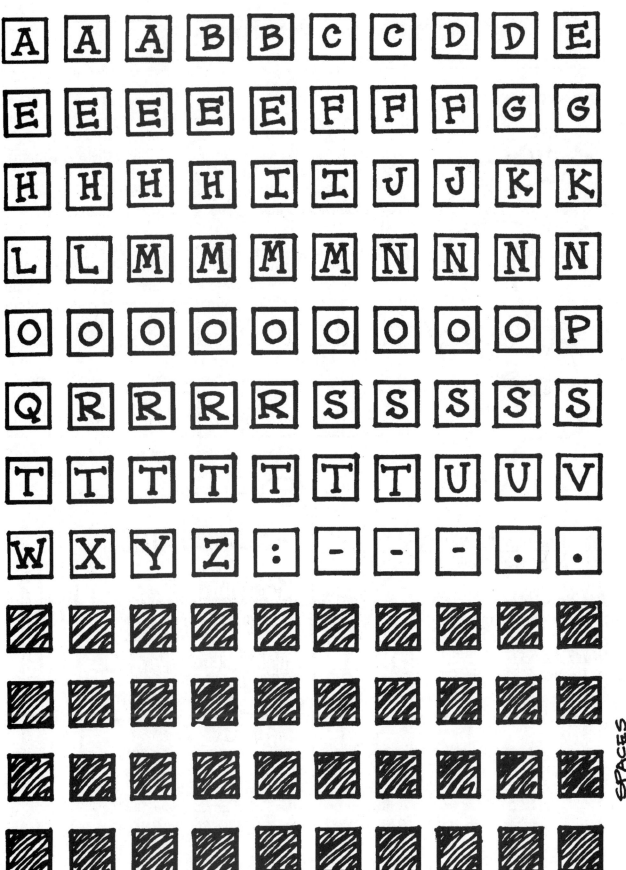

SPACES

CELESTIAL KINGDOM:
I Can Live with Heavenly Father and Jesus Again

(connected kingdoms teaching tool)

See lesson #23 in Primary 5 manual*.

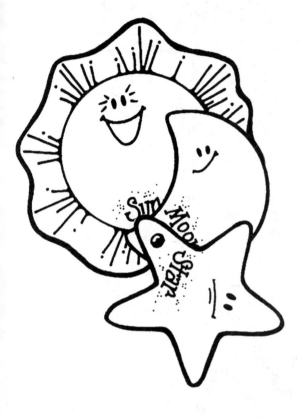

YOU'LL NEED: Copy of sun, moon, star pattern (pages 19-20) and kingdom description (below) patterns (below), SCRIPTURE CHALLENGE CARD (page 102) on colored cardstock paper, and a metal or button brad for each child, scissors, glue, paper punch, and crayons

ACTIVITY: Help children choose to live with Heavenly Father and Jesus Christ again in the Celestial Kingdom by comparing three possible places they could live after this earth life. Children can take it home and read scriptures with their family and share this teaching tool.

TO MAKE TEACHING TOOL:
1. Color and cut out the sun, moon, star, and matching kingdom descriptions.
2. Glue kingdom descriptions on back of the matching kingdom.
3. Poke a hole where indicated on sun, moon, star, and kingdoms description.
4. Place a metal or button brad through holes to attach pieces.

TO MAKE BUTTON BRAD: Sew two buttons together on opposite sides (threading thread through the same hole) to attach kingdom pieces.

SCRIPTURE CHALLENGE CARD: Assign each child a new card and reward them with a glue-on sticker for the card completed.

THOUGHT TREAT: Celestial Soda.
1. Copy (reduce 50%), color, and cut out an extra sun (page 19) for each child.
2. Punch two holes on each side and insert a straw.
3. Place straw in an 8-ounce cup filled with soda pop or punch that each child can enjoy as you say,

"As we sip this Celestial Soda, let's imagine what it would be like to live with Heavenly Father and Jesus and our families forever. We are created in Heavenly Father's image and we can become like him. Our goal is to get back to heaven to live in the Celestial Kingdom. So let's say each day, 'I AM HEAVEN SENT AND HEAVEN BOUND'"

*Primary 5 manual is published by The Church of Jesus Christ of Latter-day Saints, Salt Lake City, Utah.

CELESTIAL KINGDOM

Glory compared to brightness of the sun--<u>highest</u> kingdom (D&C 76:91). People who have been baptized and confirmed and keep the commandments will live here (D&C 76:50-52).

1. They will live with Heavenly Father and Jesus Christ <u>forever</u> (D&C 76:62).
2. Become like Heavenly Father (D&C 76:58; 132:20).
3. Live with your righteous family members* (D&C 131:2-4).
4. Receive a fulness of joy (D&C 138:17). There are three heavens or degrees in this celestial kingdom (D&C 131:1). To live in the highest kingdom one must make sacred covenants, promises, be married, and sealed to our families for eternity (D&C 131:2-3).

*The highest degree is the <u>only</u> place families can live together forever.

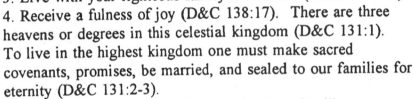

TELESTIAL KINGDOM

Glory compared to the brightness of a star-- the <u>lowest</u> kingdom. Those who did not <u>accept</u> the gospel of Christ, or have a testimony of Jesus. Liars, sorcerers, adulterers, whoremongers. Thrust down to hell, redeemed of the Lord in the last resurrection. The Holy Ghost and angels will minister to these people. They will know of Heavenly Father and Jesus but will <u>never</u> live with them or see them. *They won't be able to live with their families. D&C 76:81-103

TERRESTRIAL KINGDOM

Glory compared to the brightness of the moon--the <u>middle</u> kingdom (D&C 76:72-91). These people are those who die without law. Jesus will <u>visit</u> the people here. They will know of Heavenly Father but will <u>never</u> live with him. They do not receive a testimony of Jesus in the flesh, but after death receive a testimony. Honorable, but blinded by the craftiness of men, not valiant in the testimony of Jesus. *These people won't be able to live with their families.

COMMANDMENTS: I Will Be Blessed as I Obey and Endure to the End

(BLACKOUT! Promise Puzzle)

See lesson #27 in Primary 5 manual*.

YOU'LL NEED: Copy of promise puzzle pattern (page 22) on lightweight paper, SCRIPTURE CHALLENGE CARD (page 104) on colored cardstock paper for each child, pencils, and crayons

ACTIVITY: Challenge children to find a very special promise for keeping the commandments. Follow directions to learn the scripture found in D&C 82:10.

SCRIPTURE CHALLENGE**

THOUGHT TREAT: Testimony Treats. Tell children that as they gain a testimony of the gospel of Jesus Christ they will want to live the commandments. Tell children you will give them an M&M® candy or a grape for every commandment they write on the chalk board or on paper. If they can write down how they can obey any a commandment listed, they receive two treats. Divide into teams and set a five minute limit.

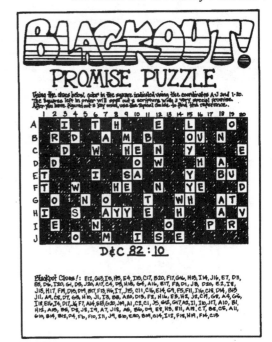

FAITH: Faith in Jesus Christ Helps Me with Problems

(Jesus Lights Up My Life light-switch cover)

See lesson #42 in Primary 5 manual*.

YOU'LL NEED: Copy of light-switch cover pattern (page 23), SCRIPTURE CHALLENGE CARD (page 111) on colored cardstock paper for each child, scissors, and crayons

ACTIVITY: Remind children with this light-switch cover that Jesus Christ lit the way for pioneers to help them solve problems, and he can light the way for us to solve our problems in these latter-days.
1. Color and cut out light-switch cover.
2. Ask children to place cover over their light-switch to remind them to have faith in Jesus Christ and he will help them with their problems.

SCRIPTURE CHALLENGE**

THOUGHT TREAT: Faith Finger Treats. Give each child five olives to place on their fingers. As they eat each olive, have them name one thing they can do to increase their faith in Jesus Christ, i.e., pray, read scriptures, attend church, pay tithing, and listen in testimony meeting.

**SCRIPTURE CHALLENGE: Assign each child a new card and reward them with a glue-on sticker for the card completed.

*Primary 5 manual is published by The Church of Jesus Christ of Latter-day Saints, Salt Lake City, Utah.

21

BLACKOUT!

PROMISE PUZZLE

Using the clues below, color in the square indicated using the coordinates A-J and 1-20. The squares left in order will spell out a scripture with a very special promise. After you have figured out a key word, use the Topical Guide to find the reference.

	1	2	3	4	5	6	7	8	9	10	11	12	13	14	15	16	17	18	19	20
A	T	B	I	L	O	T	B	H	R	I	D	E	Z	C	L	E	O	B	O	Z
B	I	R	A	D	N	R	A	M	M	O	B	O	A	N	O	U	N	N	U	N
C	N	O	D	S	R	W	A	X	H	E	S	N	O	R	Y	I	P	O	S	E
D	P	D	O	R	C	G	U	S	L	O	P	W	S	A	R	H	O	A	U	R
E	T	K	N	P	N	I	P	N	S	A	L	I	L	L	Y	L	P	B	U	T
F	T	R	Q	W	X	A	Z	H	E	A	O	N	A	R	Y	E	R	Z	O	D
G	B	O	W	D	N	B	O	C	O	N	T	U	N	W	H	T	S	A	T	A
H	I	C	O	S	O	N	A	Y	Y	V	E	V	T	H	O	X	R	A	N	V
I	L	E	L	N	D	N	U	L	N	N	U	B	O	A	R	I	P	R	R	A
J	A	H	Z	O	B	N	M	O	R	I	V	S	P	E	N	A	K	E	Y	L

D&C ___ : ___

Blackout Clues!: E12, G13, I5, H5, E4, I15, C17, B20, F17, G16, H13, I4, J16, E7, D11, E5, D6, I20, G1, D5, J20, A17, C4, D3, H15, G4, A16, E17, F3, D1, J3, D20, E2, I8, J13, H17, F19, D15, D19, B17, F13, H6, I7, J15, C11, C16, E14, G9, F5, F11, I16, C18, D14, B13, J11, A9, C8, D7, G3, H10, J1, I3, B3, A20, D13, F2, H16, E3, H2, J2, C19, G8, A4, G6, I18, E16, I4, D17, J6, F7, A14, E13, G20, J19, A1, C2, C1, J5, G12, G17, A2, I1, I10, J17, A10, B1, H12, A13, B5, D8, J8, I9, A7, J18, A5, B6, D9, E8, H3, E11, A18, C7, B8, C5, A11, G10, B14, B12, D4, F6, F10, I11, J9, B10, E20, B19, C14, I12, F18, H9, F14, C13

FAITH: I Will Rely on Heavenly Father When I Have Problems

(D&C 121:7-8 Bite-size Memorize)   See lesson #32 in Primary 5 manual*.

BITE SIZE MEMORIZE

Peace be unto thy soul; thine adversity and thine afflictions shall be but a small moment; And then if thou endure it well, God shall exalt thee on high; thou shalt triumph over all thy foes.
– D&C 121:7-8 –

YOU'LL NEED: Copy of D&C bite-size memorize pattern (page 25), SCRIPTURE CHALLENGE CARD (page 106) on colored cardstock paper for each child, pencils, and crayons
ACTIVITY: Help children memorize D&C 121:7-8 to know that they can rely on Heavenly Father when they have problems. Prayer is the key. Have faith that you will receive guidance in making decisions. Remind children to obey the commandments, so that when they are in difficult or challenging situations they can receive guidance from the Holy Ghost.
*SCRIPTURE CHALLENGE***
THOUGHT TREAT: Seeds of Faith. Give children sunflower seeds in a cup or plastic bag. Tell them that faith is like a little seed. It starts small and grows. The more we think good thoughts and pray to our Heavenly Father, the stronger our faith becomes. This feeling of faith grows in our heart and tells us that Heavenly Father loves us and will help us. He will help us during hard times if we have faith in him and keep the commandments.

FIRST VISION: Joseph Smith Saw Heavenly Father and Jesus Christ

(testimony bookmark)   See lesson #1 in Primary 5 manual*.

First Vision

YOU'LL NEED: Copy of testimony bookmark pattern (page 26) and SCRIPTURE CHALLENGE CARD (page 91) on colored cardstock paper, and a 6" ribbon or yarn for each child, scissors, paper punch, and crayons
ACTIVITY: Help children memorize the testimony of Joseph Smith that testifies of the truth Joseph Smith discovered as he knelt in the Sacred Grove. (1) Color and cut out bookmark. (2) Fold bookmark in half and glue back-to-back. (3) Paper punch a hole at top and tie a 6" ribbon through and tie a knot. (4) Have children place bookmark in their scriptures to remind them to have faith as the Prophet Joseph Smith. Remind children that he was only 14 years old when he had this sacred experience.
*SCRIPTURE CHALLENGE***
THOUGHT TREAT: Sacred Grove Cone Cakes. Pour cake batter into ice cream cone (flat on bottom) one-half full. Bake in 350° oven 20-22 minutes. Frost cupcake cones with green frosting. Green-topped cones together look like the Sacred Grove of trees where Joseph Smith knelt when he saw Heavenly Father and Jesus Christ. Tell children that they too can receive a testimony of the First Vision as they pray to Heavenly Father. Read James 1:5 and tell children that this is the scripture Joseph Smith read in the Bible that encouraged him to pray to know the truth.

**SCRIPTURE CHALLENGE: Assign each child a new card and reward them with a glue-on sticker for the card completed.

*Primary 5 manual is published by The Church of Jesus Christ of Latter-day Saints, Salt Lake City, Utah.

Peace be unto thy soul; thine adversity and thine afflictions shall be but a small moment; And then if thou endure it well, God shall exhalt thee on high; thou shalt triumph over all thy foes.

-D&C 121:7-8-

"So it was with me. I had actually seen a light, and in the midst of that light I saw two Personages, and they did in reality speak to me; and though I was hated and persecuted for saying that I had seen a vision, yet it was true; and while they were persecuting me, reviling me, and speaking all manner of evil against me falsely for so saying, I was led to say in my heart: Why persecute me for telling the truth? I have actually seen a vision; and who am I that I can withstand God, or why does the world think to make me deny what I have actually seen? For I had seen a vision; I knew it, and I knew that God knew it, and I could not deny it, neither dared I do it; at least I knew that by so doing I would offend God, and come under condemnation." —JS History 1:25

First Vision

"So it was with me. I had actually seen a light, and in the midst of that light I saw two Personages, and they did in reality speak to me; and though I was hated and persecuted for saying that I had seen a vision, yet it was true; and while they were persecuting me, reviling me, and speaking all manner of evil against me falsely for so saying, I was led to say in my heart: Why persecute me for telling the truth? I have actually seen a vision; and who am I that I can withstand God, or why does the world think to make me deny what I have actually seen? For I had seen a vision; I knew it, and I knew that God knew it, and I could not deny it, neither dared I do it; at least I knew that by so doing I would offend God, and come under condemnation." —JS History 1:25

First Vision

FORGIVENESS: I Will Forgive Others and Find Peace

(D&C 64:10 bite-size memorize)

See lesson #21 in Primary 5 manual*.

YOU'LL NEED: Copy of bite-size memorize scripture pattern (page 28), SCRIPTURE CHALLENGE CARD (page 101) on colored cardstock paper for each child, and crayons

ACTIVITY: Help children memorize Doctrine and Covenants 64:10 and talk about ways they might forgive another person. Talk about the feelings of peace they find when they forgive.

*SCRIPTURE CHALLENGE***

THOUGHT TREAT: Disappearing Candy. Give each child a buttermint or piece of hardtack candy. Tell children, "As you forgive someone who has hurt you, or someone who has made you angry, those ugly feelings will disappear just as the hard candy disappears."

GIFTS OF THE SPIRIT: I Can Recognize and Seek True Gifts

(Gifts of the Spirit cross match)

See lesson #19 in Primary 5 manual*.

YOU'LL NEED: Copy of Gifts of the Spirit cross match pattern (page 29), SCRIPTURE CHALLENGE CARD (page 100) on colored cardstock paper for each child, pencils, and crayons

ACTIVITY: Have children draw a line from the scripture to the gift (of the Spirit) found in the scripture. Talk about the gifts and why it is important to recognize and seek true gifts.

*SCRIPTURE CHALLENGE***

THOUGHT TREAT: Gift Gumdrops. Give each child six different colors of gumdrops in a bag. Ask children to name a gift of the spirit with each gumdrop they eat. Name the six gifts found in the scripture activity above: Testimony--belief in Jesus Christ (D&C 46:14), belief in testimonies of others (D&C 46:19-20), wisdom and knowledge (D&C 46:13), faith to heal and be healed (D&C 46:17-18), prophecy (D&C 46:24-25), and speaking and understanding languages (D&C 46:22).

SCRIPTURE CHALLENGE: Assign each child a new card and reward them with a glue-on sticker for the card completed.

*Primary 5 manual is published by The Church of Jesus Christ of Latter-day Saints, Salt Lake City, Utah.

27

I, the Lord, 4-give whom I 4-give, but of U it is re-quired to 4-give all.

D&C 64:10

Gifts of the Spirit

Fill in the blank and match the gift with the correct reference.

D&C 46:22

D&C 46:24-25

D&C 46:17-18

D&C 46:14

D&C 46:19-20

D&C 46:13

- Gifts of w_____ and K_____.

- Gift to _____ the testimony of others.

- Gifts of faith to_____ and be_____.

- Gift of p_____.

- Gift to_____ that Jesus is the_____.

- Gift to s____ and understand languages.

GOSPEL FULNESS: Angel Moroni's Good News Message

(Moroni's Match game)

See lesson #3 in Primary 5 manual*.

YOU'LL NEED: Copy of Moroni's Message bag label and two sets of the Moroni's Match Game cards (pages 31-32) and SCRIPTURE CHALLENGE CARD (page 92) on colored cardstock paper for each child, scissors, zip-close plastic bag, and crayons

ACTIVITY: Play Moroni's Match Game to remind children of the basic elements of the gospel. (1) Color and cut one or two sets of Moroni's Match Game cards, mix up cards and lay facedown on the floor or table. (2) Children sit in a circle to play. (3) Take turns turning two cards over for all to see and name the gospel basics. (4) When a match is made, child collects matching cards. The one with the most matches wins. Option: Divide class into two teams before playing. Storage Bag: Give each child a zip-close plastic bag to store Moroni's Match Game cards.

*SCRIPTURE CHALLENGE***

THOUGHT TREAT: Gospel Granola. Give each child a granola bar and say, "Just as granola is made up of different ingredients like oats, sugar, nuts, and raisins that make it great, so is the gospel of Jesus Christ is made up of the basic elements or ingredients to make it full and complete. The gospel ingredients are found in the match cards: Faith in Jesus Christ, Repentance, Baptism by Immersion, the Gift of the Holy Ghost, the Book of Mormon, Living Prophets, Priesthood Authority, Continuous Revelation, and Temple Ordinances."

GRATITUDE: I Will Work Hard to Serve, Like the Pioneers

(pioneer word find puzzle)

See lesson #40 in Primary 5 manual*.

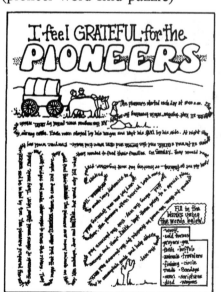

YOU'LL NEED: Copy of puzzle pattern (page 33), SCRIPTURE CHALLENGE CARD (page 110) on colored cardstock paper for each child, highlight markers or pencils, and crayons

ACTIVITY: Help children fill in the puzzle blanks using the words below to think about the struggles of the Mormon pioneers who found and settled the Salt Lake valley. Children can cross out or highlight words found as they add them to the trail of words. Remind children that the pioneers prepared the way for thousands of pioneers to come. Their hardships and hard work are described in this puzzle. Children can do this activity individually or as teams to show gratitude. The first child or team to complete wins.

*SCRIPTURE CHALLENGE***

THOUGHT TREAT: "Grape-ful" Grateful Grapes. Share grapes with children and talk about how grateful you are for the pioneers' hard work. "Grape-ful" Examples: Pioneers pulled covered wagons across the plains, built a new trail called the Mormon trail, protected themselves from Indian attacks, made friends with many Indians, fished and hunted for food, crossed large rivers and streams, traveled with horses and oxen over the rough Rocky Mountains, planted food along the way, and prepared the way for thousands of other Saints to enter the Salt Lake Valley.

**SCRIPTURE CHALLENGE: Assign each child a new card and reward them with a glue-on sticker for the card completed.

PATTERN: GOSPEL FULNESS (Moroni's Message bag label)   See lesson #3 in Primary 5 manual*.

*Primary 5 manual is published by The Church of Jesus Christ of Latter-day Saints, Salt Lake City, Utah.

I feel GRATEFUL for the PIONEERS

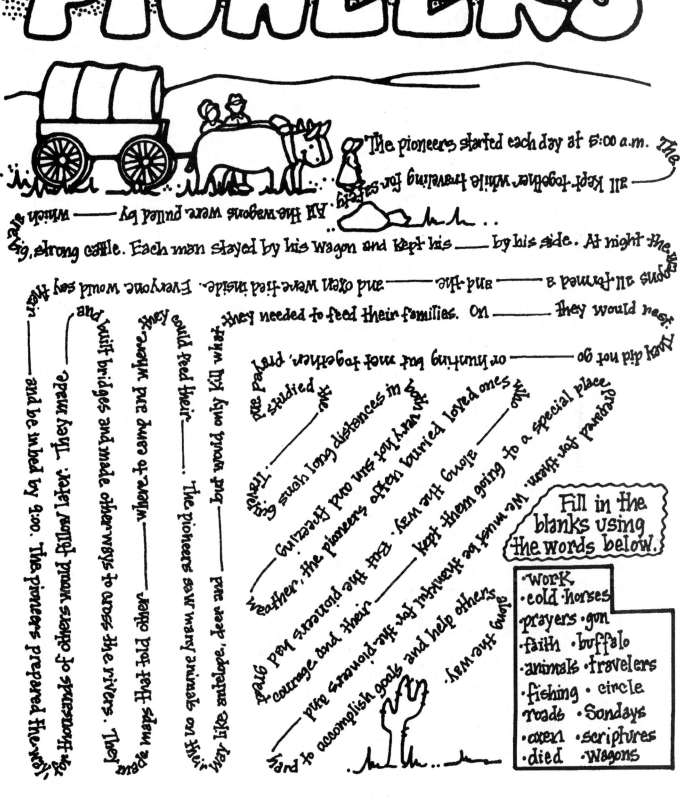

The pioneers started each day at 5:00 a.m. The _____ all kept together while traveling for safety. All the wagons were pulled by _____ which are big, strong cattle. Each man stayed by his wagon and kept his _____ by his side. At night the wagons all formed a _____ and the _____ and oxen were tied inside. Everyone would say their _____ they needed to feed their families. On _____ they would rest. They did not go _____ or hunting but met together, prayed and studied the _____. They _____ and built bridges and made otherwise. They made maps that told other _____ where to camp and where they could feed their _____. The pioneers saw many animals on their way like antelope, deer and _____ but would only kill what for thousands of others would follow later. They made _____ across the rivers. They _____ and be in bed by 9:00. The pioneers prepared the way.

Traveling such long distances in hot weather, the pioneers often buried loved ones along the way. But the pioneers had _____ who kept them going to a special place prepared for them. We must be thankful for the pioneers had courage and their _____ and faith to accomplish goals and help others and _____ along the way.

Fill in the blanks using the words below.

- work
- cold
- horses
- prayers
- gun
- faith
- buffalo
- animals
- travelers
- fishing
- circle
- roads
- Sondays
- oxen
- scriptures
- died
- wagons

HOLY GHOST: The Holy Ghost Will Guide and Comfort Me

(Invite the Spirit choice game)   See lesson #7 in Primary 5 manual*.

YOU'LL NEED: Copy of Invites the Spirit/Turns Spirit Away two-sided bag label and choice wordstrips patterns (page 35-36) and SCRIPTURE CHALLENGE CARD (page 94) on colored cardstock paper and a zip-close plastic bag for each child, scissors, and crayons

ACTIVITY: With this game children can learn of choices that invite the Spirit of the Holy Ghost and of choices that turn away the Spirit. (1) Color and cut out Invite Spirit/Turns Spirit Away two-sided bag label and choice wordstrips.
(2) Fold two-sided label and place in a zip-close plastic bag.
(3) Place choice wordstrips inside bag.

PLAY INVITE THE SPIRIT CHOICE GAME: Divide class into two teams. Take turns drawing a choice wordstrip from the bag and reading it aloud. The player makes a choice by saying, "Invites the Spirit," or "Turns away the Spirit." Each right choice is 1 point. Play 10-15 minutes or until all wordstrips are read.

*SCRIPTURE CHALLENGE**

THOUGHT TREAT: Prayer Pudding. Give each child a small package of pudding and a spoon. Have a child say a prayer to bless the food. As they eat the pudding, talk about what they can say in prayer, i.e.: Blessings they can thank Heavenly Father for, and what they might ask for. With the last bite say, "I'm sure thankful for this Prayer Pudding!"

HYMNS: The Sacred Hymns Bring Us Blessings

("Note"able Hymns secret code message)   See lesson #14 in Primary 5 manual*.

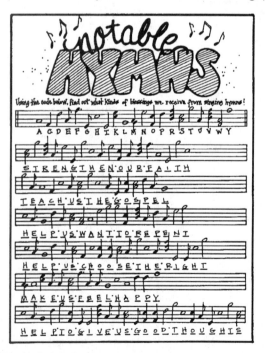

YOU'LL NEED: Copy of "Note"able Hymns secret code message pattern (page 37), SCRIPTURE CHALLENGE CARD (page 97) on colored cardstock paper, and a pencil for each child, scissors, and crayons

ACTIVITY: Using the code breaker, have children find the hidden messages that tell us the kinds of blessings we receive from singing hymns. Answers: Strengthen our faith, teach us the gospel, help us want to repent, help us choose the right, make us feel happy, and help to give us good thoughts.

*SCRIPTURE CHALLENGE**

THOUGHT TREAT: Note Cookies. Make or purchase round sugar cookies. Frost and decorate (with tube of frosting) in the shape of a musical note.

SCRIPTURE CHALLENGE: Assign each child a new card and reward them with a glue-on sticker for the card completed.

PATTERN: HOLY GHOST (Invite the Spirit Choice Game two-sided bag label)   See lesson #7 in Primary 5 manual*.

Fold - -   - -Fold

PATTERN: HOLY GHOST (Invite the Spirit Choice Game wordstrips)   See lesson #7 in Primary 5 manual*.

search the scriptures for truth	pray with real intent
get even when you feel hurt	be forgiving and kind
feel happy when others are sad	take something without asking
volunteer and help older person	thank teacher for lesson
be reverent in church	pay tithing on all money earned
take a toy away from brother	take something without paying
help brother or sister	wash dishes without being asked
watch a scary movie	tease younger sister
frighten someone	tell an untruth
miss family home evening	have family prayer
set the table for dinner	take out garbage
skip doing homework	talk bad about teacher
sass mother	talk rude about a friend
frown all day	forgive someone
go to bed late	go to be early and get up early
keep a record of your people	decide not to keep a record
told a friend you'd call but didn't	your plant died from neglect
you spent your tithing money	don't obey all the commandments
trust in others rather than Jesus	waste someone's time
don't help when needed	don't listen
care for others more than self	can't wait to read standard works
take more food than you can eat	eat too much food
skipped mission	married outside temple
told a dirty joke	saw someone steal and not tell
talked to friend in church	borrowed a pen and didn't return
feeling good/asked to go home sick	didn't go straight home/didn't call

     *Primary 5 manual is published by The Church of Jesus Christ of Latter-day Saints, Salt Lake City, Utah.

Using the code below, find out what Kinds of blessings we receive from singing hymns!

A C D E F G H I K L M N O P R S T U V W Y

LAW OF CONSECRATION: I Share to Build Up the Kingdom of God

(Consecration Checkbook)

See lesson #18 in Primary 5 manual*.

YOU'LL NEED: Copy of Consecration Checkbook patterns (page 39), SCRIPTURE CHALLENGE CARD (page 99) on colored cardstock paper for each child, scissors, stapler, and crayons

ACTIVITY: Give children a Consecration Checkbook to help consecrate or give of their time, talents, and means to build up the kingdom of God on the earth.
(1) Color and cut out checkbook. (2) Staple checkbook with Consecration Checkbook as the cover.
(3) Children fill out date and the name of the person they are giving to. On the "For" line they write what service they did (to give of their time, talents, or means). Children can report back the next week to share how they lived the law of consecration. **TIME:** Visit someone who is lonely, cheer up someone who is sad, read to a brother or sister, sweep the floor, play with baby brother, listen to someone, or babysit so parents can attend the temple. **TALENTS:** Play the piano, paint a picture, help mother lift or move heavy things, help make a quilt for someone in need, or sing baby sister to sleep. **MEANS:** Tithing, fast offering, missionary fund, or giving food and clothing to needy.
SCRIPTURE CHALLENGE*

THOUGHT TREAT: Treats to Double Share. Share a treat with the children and provide enough for each child to take home and share with someone in need.

LOVE AND UNITY: I Will Love and Help Others

(woven heart message)

See lesson #16 in Primary 5 manual*.

YOU'LL NEED: Copy of woven heart message pattern (page 40), SCRIPTURE CHALLENGE CARD (page 98) on colored cardstock paper, scissors, glue, and crayons

ACTIVITY: To help children realize they can inspire love and unity at church and in the family. (1) Cut out heart halves and cut up thin lines to weave halves together. (2) Weave and glue ends so heart will not separate. (3) Color as desired. (4) As children are weaving have them think of ways they can inspire love and unity at church and at home.
SCRIPTURE CHALLENGE*

THOUGHT TREAT: Heart-Shaped Candy or Cookies. Tell children that helping others in church and at home brings a warm feeling in your heart.

As you eat, talk about ways they can serve at church and at home to create unity and love. Share personal experiences.

**SCRIPTURE CHALLENGE: Assign each child a new card and reward them with a glue-on sticker for the card completed.

*Primary 5 manual is published by The Church of Jesus Christ of Latter-day Saints, Salt Lake City, Utah.

CONSEGRATION CHECKBOOK

TIME	Date: _____ To: _____ For: _____ Sign: _____

TALENT	Date: _____ To: _____ For: _____ Sign: _____

MEANS	Date: _____ To: _____ For: _____ Sign: _____

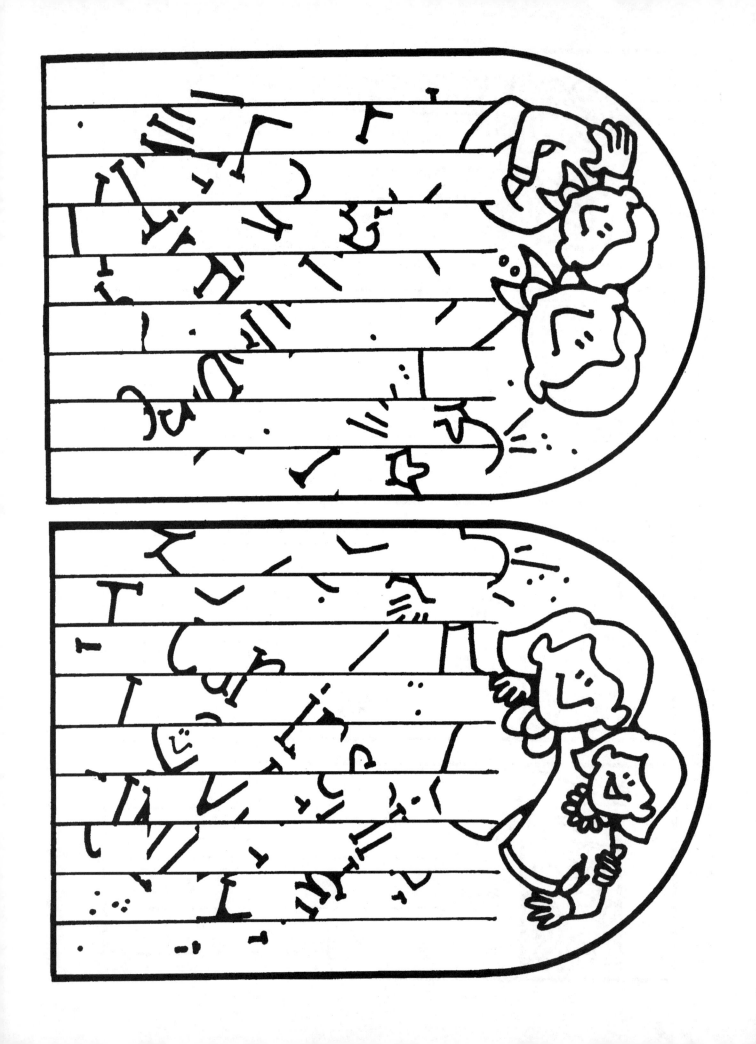

MISSIONARY: I Will Share the Gospel of Jesus Christ with Others

(bendable missionary dolls)

See lesson #13 in Primary 5 manual*.

YOU'LL NEED: Copy of girl or boy missionary pattern (pages 42-43), SCRIPTURE CHALLENGE CARD (page 97) on colored cardstock paper, and two 12" pipecleaners or wire for each child, scissors, glue, and crayons.

ACTIVITY: Create a bendable missionary doll to remind children to develop the qualities needed to be a successful missionary: Knowledge, diligence, virtue, brotherly kindness, temperance, charity, faith, godliness, and humility.

1. Color and cut out missionary girl or boy.
2. Glue pipe cleaners or tape wire down the middle to connect doll parts to bend and move in any position.
3. Bend so missionary will sit on scriptures to remind them to read them!

*SCRIPTURE CHALLENGE***

THOUGHT TREAT: Gingerbread Missionary. Roll out gingerbread cookie dough 1/2" thick and cut with people-shaped cookie cutters. Bake and frost.

MISSIONARY: I Will Share the Gospel of Jesus Christ with Others

(missionary stretch chart)

See lesson #29 in Primary 5 manual*.

YOU'LL NEED: Copy of missionary girl or boy stretch chart pattern (pages 44-45), SCRIPTURE CHALLENGE CARD (page 105) on colored cardstock paper for each child, scissors, glue or tape, and crayons

ACTIVITY: Create a missionary stretch chart to remind children they can be a missionary now. Chart shows 10 ways they can stretch their talents as a missionary.

1. Color and cut out chart.
2. Glue or tape part A to part B.

*SCRIPTURE CHALLENGE***

THOUGHT TREAT: Stretch Tall Licorice String. Give children a string of licorice and as you eat, stretch it and talk about stretching your talents to serve as a missionary. Start now to increase your missionary skills and talents, so that when you are called to serve you will be ready.

SCRIPTURE CHALLENGE: Assign each child a new card and reward them with a glue-on sticker for the card completed.

I CAN BE A MISSIONARY NOW!

10 WAYS TO STRETCH YOUR TALENTS AS A MISSIONARY!

- Learn the Articles of Faith
- Read the Scriptures
- Be a friend to those left alone.

GLUE TO A

- Read the Church magazines
- Be courteous and kind
- Learn the Church hymns
- Share my testimony of Jesus
- Be a good example to others
- Share a Church video with a friend
- Invite friends to Church activities

I CAN BE A MISSIONARY NOW!

10 WAYS TO STRETCH YOUR TALENTS AS A MISSIONARY!

- Learn the Articles of Faith
- Read the Scriptures
- Be a friend to those left alone

GLUE TO A

- Read the Church magazines
- Be courteous and kind
- Learn the Church hymns
- Share my testimony of Jesus
- Be a good example to others
- Share a Church video with a friend
- Invite friends to Church activities

OBEDIENCE: Heavenly Father Will Help Me As I Obey

(message dangler)

See lesson #5 in Primary 5 manual*.

YOU'LL NEED: Copy of message dangler pattern (page 47) and SCRIPTURE CHALLENGE CARD (page 93) on colored cardstock paper, and a 12" string for each child, scissors, and crayons

ACTIVITY:
Read with children the message on the message dangler:

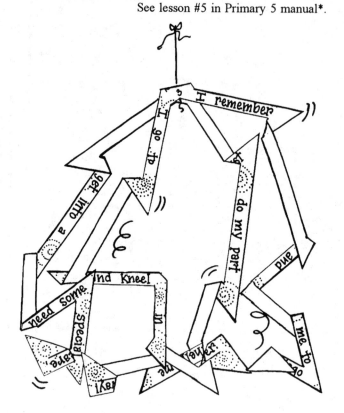

> When I get into a fix
>   and need some special care,
> I go to Heavenly Father
>   and kneel in humble prayer.
> I remember that He loves me
>   and wants me to obey.
> So I must do my part
>   and He'll help me find the way!"

This will help children know that as they obey Heavenly Father's commandments, they can ask him for help. Heavenly Father loves them and will help them find their way back to their heavenly home.

TO MAKE MESSAGE DANGLER:
1. Color message dangler.
2. Cut out dangler lines (unbroken).
3. Pierce a hole in the top with a pencil.
4. Tie a knot in a 12" string and thread through.
5. Children can hang dangler in their room.
FUN OPTION: Decorate with glitter.

SCRIPTURE CHALLENGE CARD: Assign each child a new card and reward them with a glue-on sticker for the card completed.

THOUGHT TREAT: Endure to the End Licorice
1. Give each child a string of long licorice.
2. Enjoy eating licorice to the end of the rope as you talk about enduring to the end. Ask children what they want to be or to do with their life in the next five years and beyond.
4. Read D&C 14:7 and tell children that Heavenly Father wants us to endure to the end, to obey his commandments every day of our life.

PATTERN: OBEDIENCE (message dangler)   See lesson #5 in Primary 5 manual.

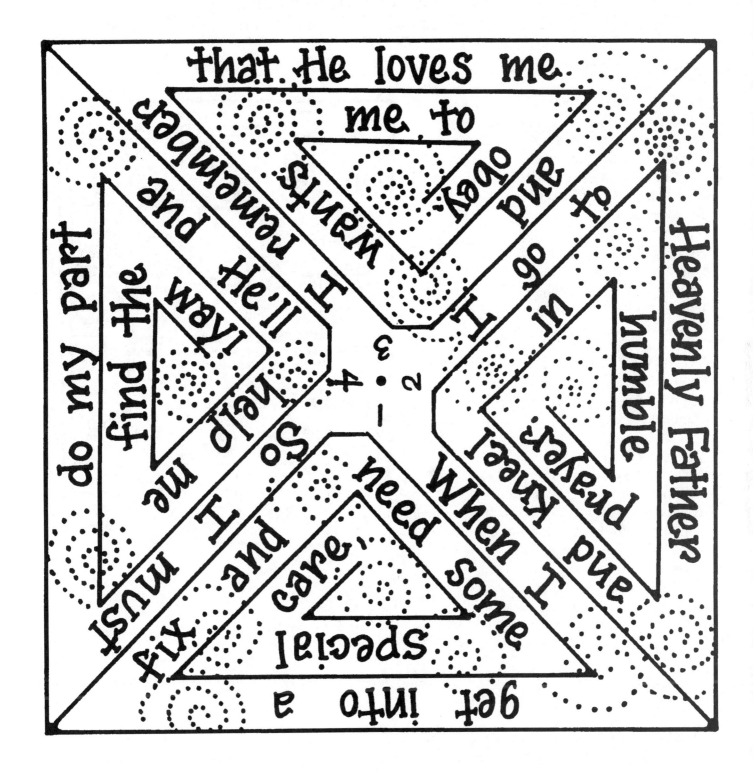

*Primary 5 manual is published by The Church of Jesus Christ of Latter-day Saints, Salt Lake City, Utah.

47

ORDINANCES RESTORED:
I'm Grateful to Be Baptized and Confirmed, and to Partake of the Sacrament

(Ordinance Opportunity game)

See lesson #12 in Primary 5 manual*.

YOU'LL NEED: Copy of Ordinance Opportunity game board, markers (candy, beans, coins), MOVE number patterns (pages 49-50), and SCRIPTURE CHALLENGE CARD (page 111) on colored cardstock paper for each child

ACTIVITY: Help children find their way back to their heavenly home by moving on the game board, trying to land on the right choices instead of the wrong.

TO MAKE GAME: Color, cut out, and laminate game board and game board markers. Cut out "MOVE" numbers 1-5 on page 50.

TO PLAY:
1. Divide class into two or four teams, selecting a marker for each team.
2. Take turns drawing MOVE numbers from a bowl or hat and moving the spaces designated from START position.
3. If you made a wrong choice move, then your team moves back instead of forward.
4. The first team to reach heaven wins!

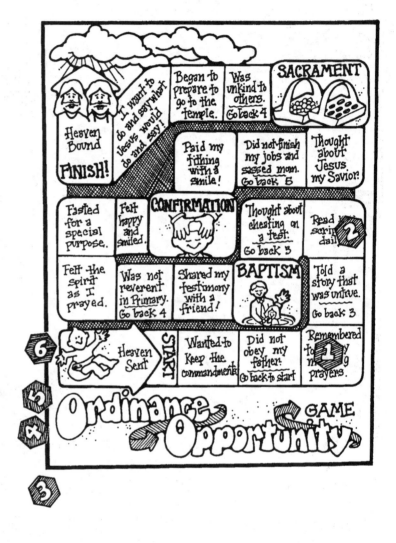

SCRIPTURE CHALLENGE CARD: Assign each child a new card and reward them with a glue-on sticker for the card completed.

THOUGHT TREAT: Ordinance Oatmeal Cookies. Prepare a half batch of oatmeal cookies without the sugar and without raisins, and prepare a batch with sugar and with raisins. First share the unsweetened cookie to children and say, "As you eat this plain cookie, without sugar and without raisins, think what your life would be like if you did not have the sweet blessings of gospel ordinances--like being baptized and then being confirmed to receive the Holy Ghost, or partaking of the sacrament to remind you of Jesus." Then share a sweet cookie with raisins and say, "Now as you eat this sweet cookie think of the sweetness of these ordinances and what joy they bring into your life."

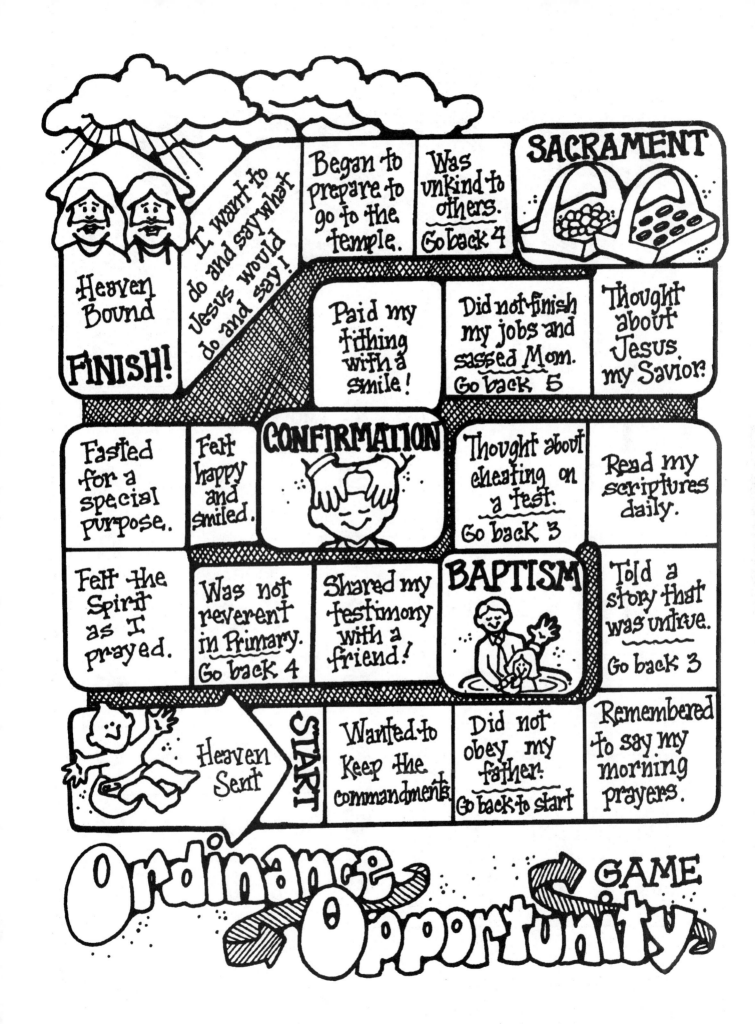

PATTERN: ORDINANCES RESTORED (markers and MOVE numbers for Ordinance Opportunity match game)

See lesson #12 in Primary 5 manual.

MOVE ①	MOVE ②	MOVE ③	MOVE ④	MOVE ⑤
MOVE ①	MOVE ②	MOVE ③	MOVE ④	MOVE ⑤
MOVE ①	MOVE ②	MOVE ③	MOVE ④	MOVE ⑤
MOVE ①	MOVE ②	MOVE ③	MOVE ④	MOVE ⑤
MOVE ①	MOVE ②	MOVE ③	MOVE ④	MOVE ⑤
MOVE ①	MOVE ②	MOVE ③	MOVE ④	MOVE ⑤
MOVE ①	MOVE ②	MOVE ③	MOVE ④	MOVE ⑤
MOVE ①	MOVE ②	MOVE ③	MOVE ④	MOVE ⑤
MOVE ①	MOVE ②	MOVE ③	MOVE ④	MOVE ⑤

*Primary 5 manual is published by The Church of Jesus Christ of Latter-day Saints, Salt Lake City, Utah.

PIONEER SPIRIT: I Will Work Hard to Leave a Legacy of Love

(Buzzzy Bee thank-you card)

See lesson #33 in Primary 5 manual*.

YOU'LL NEED: Copy of card pattern (page 52), SCRIPTURE CHALLENGE CARD (page 107) on cardstock paper and a sheet of cardstock paper for each child, scissors, glue, and crayons

ACTIVITY: Create a thank-you card children can give to a loved one to let them know that their hard work is appreciated. (1) Color and cut out card parts A and B. (2) Glue to the front and inside of a folded piece of cardstock paper. (3) Sign card and deliver or mail. (4) Encourage children to have the pioneer spirit like the hard-working Saints who settled Nauvoo. Encourage children to work hard at righteous goals so they will prosper and leave a legacy of love for their children and loved ones. Think of your parents and grandparents who have left their legacy of love, and the pioneers who unselfishly took on heavy burdens to bring us what we have today.

*SCRIPTURE CHALLENGE***

THOUGHT TREAT: Pioneer Peanut Butter Sandwich. The pioneers stuck to their beliefs just like this peanut butter sticks to this sandwich or the roof of your mouth. We too can stick to our beliefs. Each time we eat peanut butter, let's remember that if we stick to our righteous goals, Heavenly Father will stick to his promises to guide us and help us find happiness in this life and in the eternities. IDEA: Cut sandwich in a heart shape and say, "Thank you, pioneers, for your legacy of love." Tell a story of someone who had that pioneer spirit, who left a legacy of love.

PRAYER: I Will Seek Heavenly Father's Guidance

(prayer crossword puzzle)

See lesson #6 in Primary 5 manual*.

YOU'LL NEED: Copy of prayer crossword puzzle pattern (page 53) and SCRIPTURE CHALLENGE CARD (page 93) on colored cardstock paper, and a pencil for each child, and crayons

ACTIVITY: Complete this prayer crossword puzzle together to show children that answers to prayers come in many ways.

ANSWER KEY: ACROSS: 5—Heavenly Father, 7—ask, 8—morning, 9—listen, 10—thank, 15—still small voice, 17—help. DOWN: 1—Holy Ghost, 2—prayer, 3—Jesus Christ, 4—yes, 6—guidance, 11—knees, 12—night, 13—blessings, 14—no, 18—peace.

*SCRIPTURE CHALLENGE***

THOUGHT TREAT: Prayer Popcorn. Provide a bowl of popcorn children can munch on. Each time they take a handful they can tell something they might ask Heavenly Father for or thank him for. Tell children that just as heat warms kernels of corn before they pop, prayer warms our heart and messages from the Holy Ghost can "pop" into our mind.

**SCRIPTURE CHALLENGE: Assign each child a new card and reward them with a glue-on sticker for the card completed.

You're such a
buzzzy bee...

...Here's a
THANKS
from me!

Your hard work is appreciated!

Puzzled about Prayer?

Across

5. a parent (2 words)
7. request
8. early day
9. to hear
10. show gratitude
15. speaks to heart and mind (3 words)
17. aid

Down

1. invisible friend
2. kneeling activity
3. elder brother
4. affirmative
6. direction
11. prayer bones
12. day's companion
13. count them
14. negative
16. the last word
18. war's opposite

PREPARE: I Will Prepare to Serve Jesus and Others

(Prepare or Beware! maze)

See lesson #4 in Primary 5 manual*.

YOU'LL NEED: Copy of maze pattern (page 55) and SCRIPTURE CHALLENGE CARD (page 92) on colored cardstock paper for each child, scissors, and crayons

ACTIVITY: Remind children that Jesus and others need their help. Ask them if they are ready to serve, and warn them to Prepare or Beware! Don't get caught going in the wrong direction! Learn how to prepare by working through this maze.

*SCRIPTURE CHALLENGE***

THOUGHT TREAT: Preparation Pickles. Give each child a pickle to eat and tell them, "Don't get yourself into a pickle ... Be prepared." Explain that getting yourself into a pickle is getting into a bad situation. Jesus and Heavenly Father want us to be prepared by living the commandments.

PRIESTHOOD BLESSINGS: I Will Be Worthy

(Priesthood Power Search! word search puzzle)

See lesson #8 in Primary 5 manual*.

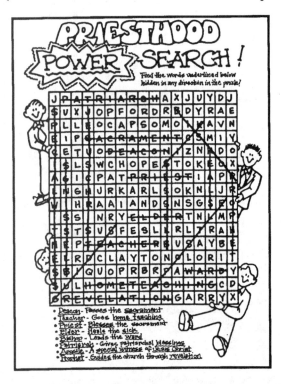

YOU'LL NEED: Copy of Priesthood Power Search pattern (page 56) and SCRIPTURE CHALLENGE CARD (page 93) on colored cardstock paper, and pencil for each child, and crayons

ACTIVITY: Find the duties and various offices in the Aaronic and Melchizedek Priesthood with this Priesthood Power word search puzzle. Cross through words/duties as you find them in' any direction.

*SCRIPTURE CHALLENGE***

THOUGHT TREAT: Priesthood Pretzels. Give each child a circular–shaped pretzels, one for each priesthood office to be discussed (for Deacon, Teacher, Priest, Elder, etc). As children eat pretzels, talk about each priesthood office and the duties for each.

SCRIPTURE CHALLENGE: Assign each child a new card and reward them with a glue-on sticker for the card completed.

PRIESTHOOD POWER SEARCH!

Find the words underlined below hidden in any direction in the puzzle!

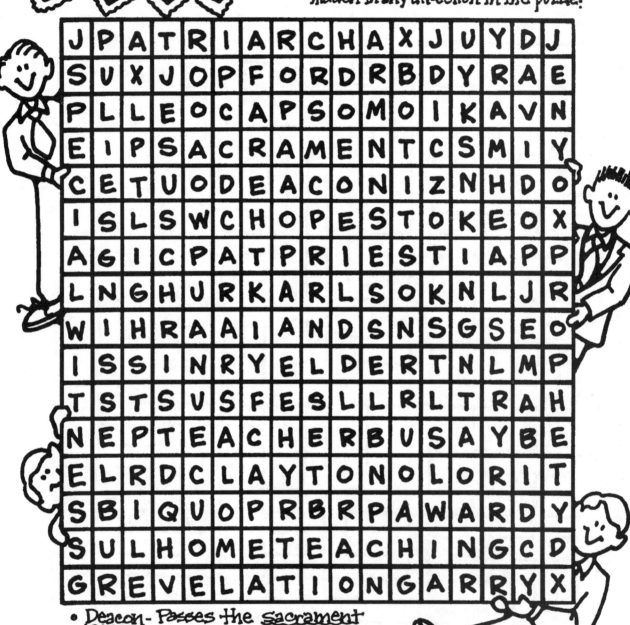

```
J P A T R I A R C H A X J U Y D J
S U X J O P F O R D R B D Y R A E
P L L E O C A P S O M O I K A V N
E I P S A C R A M E N T C S M I Y
C E T U O D E A C O N I Z N H D O
I S L S W C H O P E S T O K E O X
A G I C P A T P R I E S T I A P P
L N G H U R K A R L S O K N L J R
W I H R A A I A N D S N S G S E O
I S S I N R Y E L D E R T N L M P
T S T S V S F E S L L R L T R A H
N E P T E A C H E R B U S A Y B E
E L R D C L A Y T O N O L O R I T
S B I Q U O P R B R P A W A R D Y
S U L H O M E T E A C H I N G C D
G R E V E L A T I O N G A R R Y X
```

- **Deacon** - Passes the <u>sacrament</u>
- **Teacher** - Goes <u>home teaching</u>
- **Priest** - Blesses the <u>sacrament</u>
- **Elder** - Heals the <u>sick</u>
- **Bishop** - Leads the <u>ward</u>
- **Patriarch** - Gives patriarchal blessings
- **Apostle** - A special <u>witness</u> of Jesus Christ
- **Prophet** - Guides the Church through <u>revelation</u>

PRIESTHOOD KEYS Unlock the Powers from Heaven

(priesthood keys doorknob reminder)

See lesson #26 in Primary 5 manual*.

YOU'LL NEED: Copy of doorknob reminder pattern pieces (page 58), SCRIPTURE CHALLENGE CARD (page 103) on colored cardstock paper, and a 12" string for each child, scissors, and crayons

ACTIVITY: Remind children that Joseph Smith and Oliver Cowdery unlocked the powers of heaven when they received the priesthood keys from the prophets Moses and Elijah.

TO MAKE KEYS: (1) Read the scriptures on each key to know who restored which priesthood key, Moses or Elijah. (2) Cut out the Moses and Elijah figures and glue on the right key. (3) Glue keys back-to-back. (4) Punch a hole in key and tie a 12" string. Attach keys to your bedroom door to remind you of the priesthood keys that will unlock the powers of heaven.

*SCRIPTURE CHALLENGE***

THOUGHT TREAT: Cloud 9 Pudding. Serve, pudding topped with whipped cream to remind children that the cloud 9 feeling or feeling close to heaven can come whenever we remember the priesthood power to do missionary and temple work. Missionary work means that others will learn of the gospel of Jesus Christ, and temple work means that those living and dead can be sealed to be with their families forever.

PROPHET GUIDES: I Will Listen to the Prophet and Obey

(Choice Consequence cross match)

See lesson #31 in Primary 5 manual*.

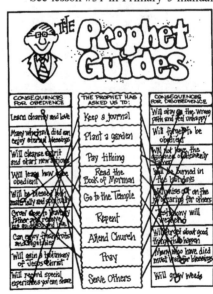

YOU'LL NEED: Copy of cross match pattern (page 59), SCRIPTURE CHALLENGE CARD (page 106) on colored cardstock paper for each child, pencils, and crayons

ACTIVITY: Help children realize the good and bad consequences that come from our choices by doing the Choice Consequence cross match. **HOW:** Draw an arrow from the action the prophet has asked us to do to the left and right side. The left side shows good consequences that come from obeying. The right side shows bad consequences that come from not obeying the prophet. Explain to children that there is always a good or bad consequence for our decisions to listen to or reject the words of the living prophet.

*SCRIPTURE CHALLENGE***

THOUGHT TREAT: Prophet Speaks and I Listen Cookie Crunch. Serve children cookies to crunch on as you read a message from the latest *Ensign* magazine (a message from the prophet or his counselors).

**SCRIPTURE CHALLENGE: Assign each child a new card and reward them with a glue-on sticker for the card completed.

*Primary 5 manual and Ensign magazine are published by The Church of Jesus Christ of Latter-day Saints, Salt Lake City, Utah.

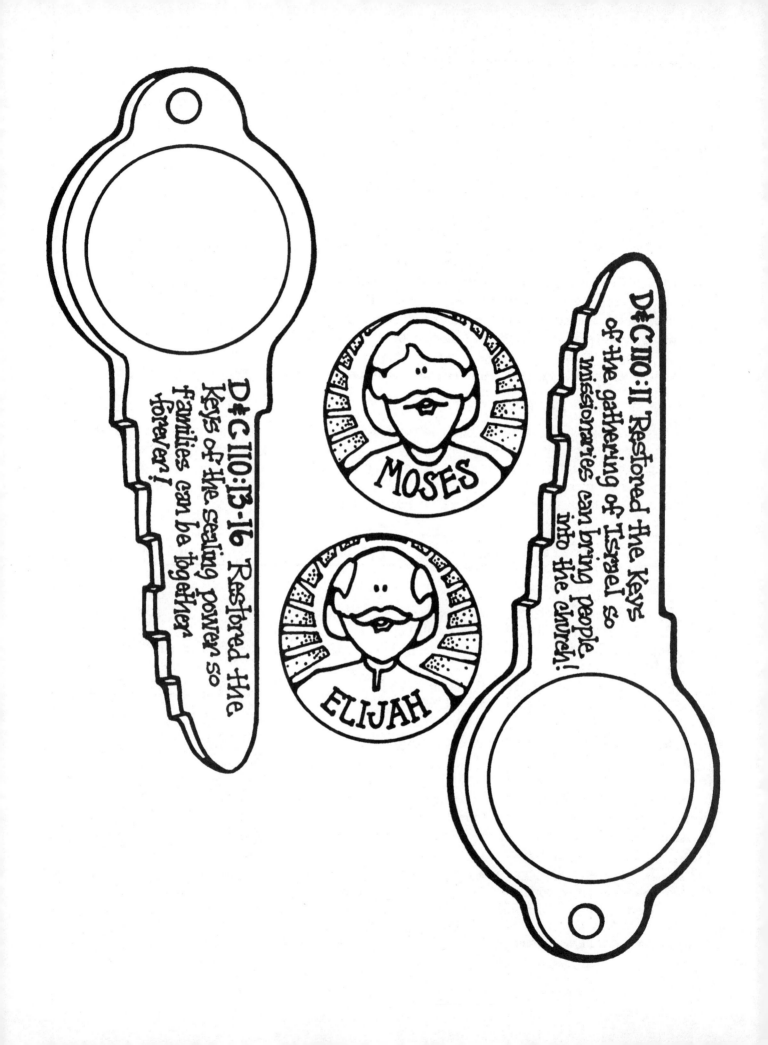

D&C 110:13-16 Restored the keys of the sealing power so families can be together forever!

MOSES

ELIJAH

D&C 110:11 Restored the keys of the gathering of Israel so missionaries can bring people into the church!

THE Prophet Guides

Draw an arrow from the action (center) to the consequences for obedience (left) and the consequences for disobedience (right). Remember to follow the prophet!

CONSEQUENCES FOR OBEDIENCE	THE PROPHET HAS ASKED US TO:	CONSEQUENCES FOR DISOBEDIENCE
Learn charity and love	Keep a journal	Will stay on the wrong path and feel unhappy
Many who have died can enjoy eternal blessings	Plant a garden	Will forget to be obedient
Will cleanse spirit and start new actions	Pay tithing	Will not have the guidance of Heavenly Father
Will learn how to be obedient	Read the Book of Mormon	Will be burned in the last days
Will be blessed both materially and spiritually	Go to the Temple	Will miss out on the joy of caring for others
Grow close to Heavenly Father and receive his guidance and love.	Repent	Testimony will weaken
Can enjoy fresh fruits and vegetables	Attend Church	Will forget about good things that happen
Will gain a testimony of Jesus Christ	Pray	Many who have died must wait for blessings
Will record special experiences you can share	Serve Others	Will grow weeds

PROPHET JOSEPH SMITH Restored the Gospel of Jesus Christ

(Tribute to Joseph Smith scripture achievement search)

See lesson #37 in Primary 5 manual*.

YOU'LL NEED: Copy of scripture achievement search pattern (page 61), SCRIPTURE CHALLENGE CARD (page 109) on colored cardstock paper for each child, scissors, and crayons

ACTIVITY: John Taylor made a statement about Joseph Smith to remind us of the prophet's achievements (see D&C 135:3). Children can search this lengthy scripture to find and circle qualities they would like to emulate in their own lives. (1) On the worksheet there are some achievements missing. Ask children to fill in the blanks to complete the scripture. (2) Encourage children to tape tribute to their wall next to their bed to remind them of the achievements of this great man.

SCRIPTURE CHALLENGE**

THOUGHT TREAT: Sparkling Juice. Share with children some sparkling apple juice or orange juice (mix 7-up®--clear soda pop with juice). Tell children that just as this sparkling soda pop adds flavor to the juice, we too can add flavor to our testimonies by adding the sparkling example of Joseph Smith to our list of scripture heros.

PROPHET OF TODAY Was Called By God to Lead Us

(Zion or Bust! handcart checklist)

See lesson #38 in Primary 5 manual*.

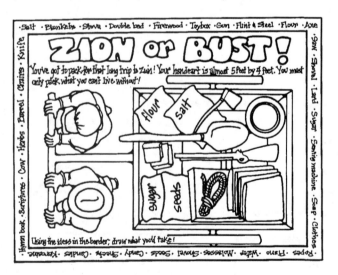

YOU'LL NEED: Copy of Zion or Bust! handcart checklist pattern (page 62), SCRIPTURE CHALLENGE CARD (page 109) on colored cardstock paper for each child, pencils, and crayons

ACTIVITY: Help children think ahead, just as the Mormon pioneers had to measure and plan what they would take in their 5 foot by 4 foot handcart. The pioneers were lead by the Prophet Brigham Young to the Salt Lake Valley. Choose from the items written in the boarder and draw inside and outside the handcart what they would take to Zion.

SCRIPTURE CHALLENGE**

THOUGHT TREAT: Hit the Trail Treats.

Dried fruits, vegetables, jerky, and water were taken along the pioneer trail.

**SCRIPTURE CHALLENGE: Assign each child a new card and reward them with a glue-on sticker for the card completed.

**Primary 5 manual is published by The Church of Jesus Christ of Latter-day Saints, Salt Lake City, Utah.

Joseph Smith
God's chosen prophet

• Look up the scripture below and find the words that will fill in the blanks.

Joseph Smith, the _____ and _____ of the Lord, has done more, save Jesus only, for the _____ of men in this _____, than any other _____ that ever lived in it. In the short space of _____ years, he has brought forth the _____ of _____, which he _____ by the _____ and _____ of God, and has been the means of _____ it on _____ continents; has sent the _____ of the everlasting _____, which it contained, to the _____ quarters of the _____; has brought forth the _____ and _____ which compose this book of _____ and _____, and many other _____ documents and _____ for the _____ of the _____ of men; _____ many _____ of the Latter-day Saints, founded a great _____, and left a fame and _____ that cannot be _____. He lived _____, and he died _____ in the _____ of _____ and his people; and like most of the Lord's _____ in _____ times, has _____ his _____ and his works with his own _____.

D&C 135:3

ZION or BUST!

You've got to pack for that long trip to Zion! You're handcart is almost 5 feet by 4 feet. You must only pack what you can't live without!

Using the ideas in the border, draw what you'd take!

Border items (clockwise from top): Hymn book • Scriptures • Cow • Herbs • Barrel • Chairs • Knife • Salt • Blankets • Stove • Double bed • Firewood • Toybox • Gun • Flint & Steel • Flour • Axe • Saw • Shovel • Land • Sugar • Sewing machine • Soap • Clothes • Ropes • Piano • Water • Molasses • Shovel • Seeds • Candy • Sheets • Candles • Kerosine

RESTORATION: The True Church Was Restored to the Earth

(*Then* and *Now* match game)

See lesson #11 in Primary 5 manual*.

First Vision

YOU'LL NEED: Copy two sets of *Then* and *Now* match game card patterns (page 64) and SCRIPTURE CHALLENGE CARD (page 96) on colored cardstock paper, a zip-close plastic bag for each child, scissors, glue, and crayons

ACTIVITY: To help children compare the gospel of Jesus Christ *then* (when Jesus came to earth), and *now* (when Joseph Smith restored the gospel in these latter days). Explain to the children the following:

Then—Sermon on the Mount
(Christ begins his ministry),

Now—First Vision
(Christ restores his Church to the earth),

Then—Jesus Ordained Apostles
(so apostles could administer the priesthood),

Now—Melchizedek Priesthood Restored
(so priesthood power can again be on the earth), and more.

1. Color and cut one or two sets of Then and Now match game cards, mix up cards and lay facedown on the floor or table.
2. Children sit in a circle to play.
3. Take turns turning two cards over for all to see, saying "then" and/or "now" as they read: Baptism by immersion ("then/now"), the last supper ("then"), sacrament ("now"), etc.
4. When a match is made, child can collect matching cards. The one with the most matches wins. Option: Divide class into two teams before playing.

STORAGE BAG: Give each child a zip-close plastic bag to store their own set of Then and Now match game cards to play and explain for family home evening.

SCRIPTURE CHALLENGE CARD: Assign each child a new card and reward them with a glue-on sticker for the card completed.

THOUGHT TREAT: Gospel Blessings Treat. Give each child a circular treat (Lifesavers® candy, Fruit Loops®, circular candy, or dried fruit rings) to munch on as you talk about gospel blessings. Talk about the circle in the circular treat and compare it to the gospel of Jesus Christ (with note below). OPTION: Copy, cut out, and hole punch note below and attach to treat.

God's eternal plan for <u>happiness</u> goes on and on, just like this <u>round</u> treat. It was God's plan in the beginning before we came to earth. And it will be God's plan forever.
The gospel of Jesus Christ was brought to the people *then*—in the days Jesus was on the earth, and *now*—to Joseph Smith in the latter days.

*Primary 5 manual is published by The Church of Jesus Christ of Latter-day Saints, Salt Lake City, Utah.

63

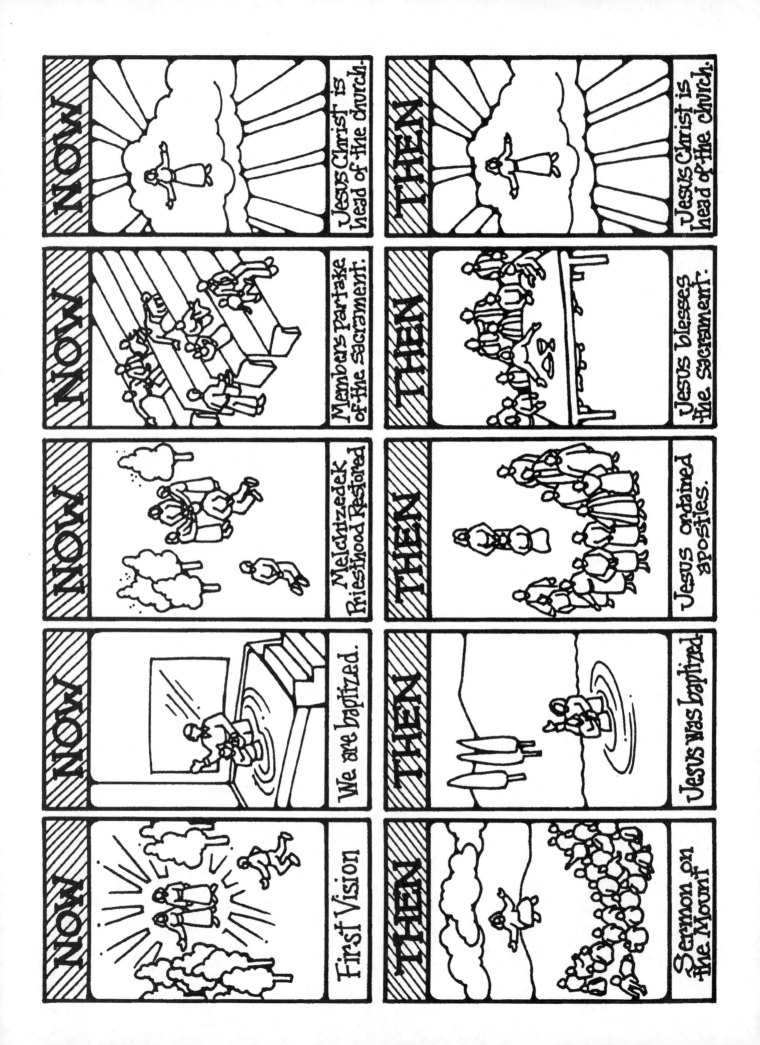

REVELATION: The Prophet Speaks and I Listen

(Revelation Routes)

See lesson #15 in Primary 5 manual*.

YOU'LL NEED: Copy of Revelation Routes pattern (page 66), SCRIPTURE CHALLENGE CARD (page 98) on colored cardstock paper, and a pencil for each child, and crayons

ACTIVITY: Have children draw an arrow to who ever receives revelation for whom, (e.g., the prophet receives revelation for the whole church so draw a line from the prophet to everyone but the Holy Ghost and Heavenly Father).

*SCRIPTURE CHALLENGE***

THOUGHT TREAT: Revelation Pretzels. Purchase or make long straight and twisted pretzel shapes. As children eat long straight pretzels remind them that the prophet reveals to us ways we can follow the straight and narrow path back to heaven. As children eat the twisted pretzels remind them that without the prophet to guide us we might get off the straight and narrow path and become lost. Say, "Let's listen to the prophet's voice to stay on the path, to gain Eternal Life and live with Heavenly Father again."

REVELATION: The Prophets Give Latter-day Revelation

(Standard Works Think-athon)

See lesson #22 in Primary 5 manual*.

YOU'LL NEED: Copy of standard works Think-athon block (to use as a die for game) and quiz wordstrips (pages 67-68) and Think-athon rules below, SCRIPTURE CHALLENGE CARD (page 101) on colored cardstock paper, and a zip-close plastic bag for each child, scissors, crayons, and tape

ACTIVITY: Color, cut-out block and quiz wordstrips. Fold box and glue tabs inside. Place wordstrips inside plastic bag. Help children learn the purpose for each of the Standard Works with a Scripture Think-athon.

SCRIPTURE THINK-ATHON RULES: (1) Divide players into two teams with one team member at a time representing their team.

(2) Teams take turns, one team member at a time answering the question.

(3) Leader draws a wordstrip and reads the think-athon question.

(4) Each team member has 10 seconds to answer the question by guessing Book of Mormon, Pearl of Great Price, Doctrine and Covenants, or the Bible, or the question will be given to the other team.

(5) If team member answers question correctly he/she may roll the die to win points for their team. The roll of the dice must match the answer to the question to receive 1 point for their team. For example, if the answer is Bible, they must roll Bible. Or if they roll "bonus" they receive 2 points. If they roll "roll again" they get another chance to win a point. (6) The team with the most points wins.

*SCRIPTURE CHALLENGE***

THOUGHT TREAT: Footstep Graham Crackers. Frost a footprint on top of a graham cracker. Tell children that if they read the scriptures they will learn how to follow in the footsteps of Jesus. Read 1 Nephi 3:7 and tell children that the Lord will prepare a way for us to obey the commandments, and to follow in his steps, that will lead us on the straight and narrow path back to heaven.

**SCRIPTURE CHALLENGE: Assign children a new card and reward them with a glue-on sticker for the card completed.

Me!

Heavenly Father & Jesus Christ

Bishop

Primary Teacher

Mom & Dad

Prophet

The Ward

Brother & Sister

Revelation Routes!

PATTERN: REVELATION (Standard Works Think-athon block—use as a die for game)   See lesson #22 in Primary 5 manual*.

PATTERN: REVELATION (Standard Works Think-athon quiz wordstrips)   See lesson #22 in Primary 5 manual*.

Which book tells us about the prophecies of Jesus Christ. Answer: Bible	Which book contains the sacrament prayers? Answer: Doctrine and Covenants
Which book tells about the Savior's life and teachings when he was on the earth. Answer: Bible	Which book tells of the restoration of the Aaronic Priesthood by John the Baptist? Answer: D&C
Which book is another testament of Jesus Christ Answer: Book of Mormon	Which book tells of qualities of a missionary? Answer: Doctrine and Covenants
Which book tells about the Savior's dealings with the people in the American continent. Answer: Book of Mormon	Which book tells of the prophet receiving revelation for the whole church? Answer: Doctrine and Covenants
Which book is a collection of revelations from Jesus Christ for the latter days, or our times. Answer: Doctrine and Covenants	Which book tells these stories: Jonah and the Whale, David and Goliath, and Shadrach, Meshach, and Abednego? Answer: Bible
Which book gives us teachings and testimonies of Jesus Christ from ancient prophets as well as Joseph Smith's history and testimony of Heavenly Father and Jesus Christ. Answer: Pearl of Great Price	Which book tells the stories of Adam and Eve, Noah and the Ark, Joseph Sold into Egypt, The Ten Commandments, and Queen Ester? Answer: Bible
Which book tells more about the Lord and his people in the Holy Land, beginning with the earth creation? Answer: Bible	Which book told the stories of Alma the Younger and Amulek, Peace in America, Crossing the Sea to the Promised land? Answer: Book of Mormon
Which book tells of Jesus Christ visiting the people on the American continent? Answer: Book of Mormon	Which book tells of Enos, King Benjamin, Abinadi and King Noah, Helaman and the 2,000 Young Men? Answer: Book of Mormon
Which book tells the most about the birth of Jesus and his life on earth? Answer: Bible	Which book tells of the three kingdoms of Heaven? Answer: Doctrine and Covenants
Which book is a record of Heavenly Father and Jesus Christ appearing to Joseph Smith in the Sacred Grove? Answer: Pearl of Great Price	Which book contains translations of the book of Matthew (found in the Bible)—by Joseph Smith? Answer: Pearl of Great Price
Which book tells how the Church should be established in the last days? Answer: Doctrine and Covenants	Which book contains translations from the ancient writings of Abraham? These records were found in the catacombs of Egypt. Answer: Pearl of G. Price
All of the standard works testify of Jesus Christ. Which one testifies of Jesus Christ visiting people in Ancient America? Answer: Book of Mormon	Which book contains the Book of Moses (parts of the Bible) translated by Joseph Smith? Answer: Pearl of Great Price
Which book tells about the Word of Wisdom? Answer: Doctrine and Covenants	Which book contains the Articles of Faith? Answer: Pearl of Great Price

     *Primary 5 manual is published by The Church of Jesus Christ of Latter-day Saints, Salt Lake City, Utah.

SABBATH DAY: I Will Keep the Sabbath Day Holy

(Sabbath Day Decision Drama or Draw)

See lesson #41 in Primary 5 manual*.

YOU'LL NEED: Copy of jar label and wordstrips (pages 70-71) on lightweight paper, SCRIPTURE CHALLENGE CARD (page 111) on colored cardstock paper for each child, scissors, and a jar

ACTIVITY: Help children learn the difference between right and wrong Sabbath Day activities. Cut out "Yes" and "No" wordstrips and place in a jar.

DECISION DRAMA OR DRAW: Children can play this by dividing into teams sitting across from the opposing team. Take turns drawing a wordstrip from a jar and reading it silently.

      OPTION #1 DRAMA: Act out the activity.

      OPTION #2 DRAW: Draw activity on the chalkboard.

The first team to guess the activity and vote "yes" (good Sabbath activity) or vote "no" (not a good Sabbath activity) wins a point for their team. Play, voting on all wordstrips or until time runs out.

SCRIPTURE CHALLENGE

THOUGHT TREAT: Sabbath Day Scripture Squiggles. Make cheese squiggles (wavy lines) on soda crackers or frosting squiggles (wavie lines) on graham crackers to remind children of a favorite Sabbath Day activity ... that of reading the scriptures.

SACRIFICE: Heavenly Father Blesses Me When I Sacrifice

(giving oyster mirror motivator)

See lesson #25 in Primary 5 manual*.

YOU'LL NEED: Copy of giving oyster mirror motivator pattern (page 72), SCRIPTURE CHALLENGE CARD (page 103) on colored cardstock paper for each child, scissors, and crayons

ACTIVITY: Create this fun giving oyster mirror motivator for each child to encourage them to be giving instead of being selfish ("shell"fish). (1) Color and cut out oyster patterns. (2) Crease shell lines to create a 3-D effect. (3) Cut slits in A and B to attach oyster to shell. (4) Glue oyster pieces together as indicated except for tab B. (5) Insert tabs where indicated and glue in place. (6) Giving means that you give up something you want to help others, i.e., your time, your talents, and your means (see lesson #18--Law of Consecration, page 38 for review).

SCRIPTURE CHALLENGE

THOUGHT TREAT: Sacrifice Soda Crackers. Serve children oyster crackers (round soda crackers), and tell them that it took sacrifice to make this soda cracker: TIME and TALENT mix ingredients, bake, cut, and package the cracker, and MEANS (money) to buy the flour, soda, and salt. Just as this soda cracker was made to eat and enjoy, we too can use our TIME, TALENTS, and MEANS to serve and help others.

**SCRIPTURE CHALLENGE: Assign each child a new card and reward them with a glue-on sticker for the card completed.

PATTERN: SABBATH DAY (Decision Drama or Draw)

See lesson #41 in Primary 5 manual*.

*Primary 5 manual is published by The Church of Jesus Christ of Latter-day Saints, Salt Lake City, Utah.

PATTERN: SABBATH DAY (Drama or Draw wordstrips)   See lesson #41 in Primary 5 manual*.

Shop for groceries	NO	Watch church video	YES
Take the dog for a walk	YES	Read church magazines	YES
Write letters	YES	Read a scripture story	YES
Visit the sick	YES	Put on a scripture play	YES
Go skiing	NO	Mop the floor	NO
Ride your bike	NO	Read brother or sister a story . . .	YES
Play with friends	NO	Listen to spiritual music	YES
Pay your tithing	YES	Help prepare a meal	YES
Go to church	YES	Read a book the prophet wrote . .	YES
Visit with family	YES	Play games with the family	YES
Have a family party	YES	Have family prayer	YES
Read the scriptures	YES	Color a picture	YES
Have family home evening	YES	Make a craft	YES
Do the dishes	YES	Write in your journal	YES
Clean the house	NO	Take notes in church	YES
Mow the lawn	NO	Listen to your teacher	YES
Clean the garage	NO	Participate in Primary	YES
Wash the car	NO	Sit reverently in church	YES
Suntan	NO	Visit grandparents	YES
Go swimming	NO	Invite a friend to church	YES
Eat out at a restaurant	NO	Do a kind deed	YES
Make a card for someone	YES	Brush the cat or dog	YES
Make your bed	YES	Talk to your brother or sister . . .	YES
Play the piano	YES	Go for a short walk	YES
Sing	YES	Take a nap	YES
Go fishing	NO	Bake cookies	YES
Play sports	NO	Help set the table	YES

PATTERN: SACRIFICE (giving oyster motivator)   See lesson #25 in Primary 5 manual*.

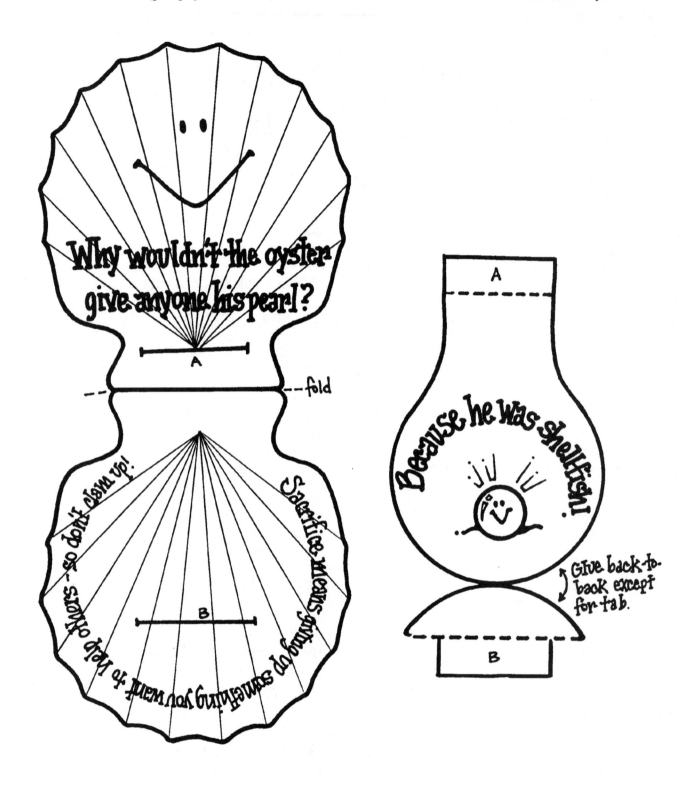

*Primary 5 manual is published by The Church of Jesus Christ of Latter-day Saints, Salt Lake City, Utah.

SCRIPTURES: I Love to Study the Scriptures

(scattered scriptures mix-and-match)

See lesson #20 in Primary 5 manual*.

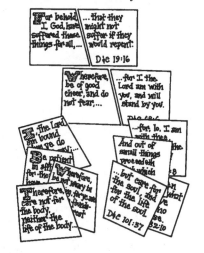

YOU'LL NEED: Copy of cards with divided scriptures patterns (pages 74-76), SCRIPTURE CHALLENGE CARD (page 100) on colored cardstock paper for each child, and crayons

ACTIVITY: Increase a child's love for the scriptures with this scattered scripture mix-and-match game. But watch out! These dual match cards may fool you, i.e. the "if ye love me" card could also match with the "bring to pass the immortality and eternal life of man" card, but it doesn't. It matches with the "keep my commandments" card. (1) Color and cut out cards. (2) Mix up cards in two separate piles face down on the table or floor. Pile #1: Beginning--scripture cards with the CAPITAL letters on the left facedown. Pile #2: Ending--scripture cards with the reference on the right facedown. (3) Take turns picking up two cards (one from each pile) to see if you can make a scripture match.

SCRIPTURE CHALLENGE**

THOUGHT TREAT: Standard Works Bite-size Cookies. Frost graham crackers or wafer type cookies together stacking four cookies on top of each other with frosting (for display only). Show this to children and compare this stack of four cookies as the four standard works: Bible, Book of Mormon, Doctrine and Covenants, and Pearl of Great Price. Tell children if they tried to eat the cookies stacked together it would be hard to do, or if they tried to read the entire standard works in one year it would be hard. Give the children four different cookies to eat one at a time. The scriptures are like eating an elephant. If you read them every day, a bite at a time, you can eat an elephant, or read the entire standard works. Read the scriptures daily and try not to rush through them. Pray about them before and after you read so the spirit of the Holy Ghost will touch your heart and witness to you of the truthfulness of what you read.

SECOND COMING: I Will Prepare to Meet My Savior Jesus Christ

(strong heart mobile)

See lesson #30 in Primary 5 manual*.

YOU'LL NEED: Copy of strong heart mobile pattern (page 77) on two different colors so one side is one color and other side is another color, SCRIPTURE CHALLENGE CARD (page 105) on colored cardstock paper, and a 2' piece of string for each child, scissors, glue, tape, and crayons

ACTIVITY: Remind children that if their thoughts are centered around Jesus Christ, keeping him in their heart at all times they will be ready when he comes again. Build a mobile to show ways they can be strong. (1) Copy on two different colors (see above). (2) Color and cut out hearts. (3) Lay the "My ♥ will not ..." side down 1/2" apart. (4) Place a 2' string down the center and tape to strips (still 1/2" apart). (5) Glue second set of heart strips to the first set of heart strips (that are face down--words facing out). Parts move left and right to hang in child's room. _SCRIPTURE CHALLENGE**_

THOUGHT TREAT: Heart Shaped Candy. Cinnamon hearts or gummy hearts to share. Tell children, "If your heart is honest (wanting to keep the commandments) you will find a peaceful warm feeling in their heart."

**SCRIPTURE CHALLENGE: Assign each child a new card and reward them with a glue-on sticker for the card completed.

Faith is not ...Therefore if ye have faith ye hope for things which are not seen, which are true. Alma 32:21

to have a perfect knowledge of things;...

Verily, verily, I say unto you, ye must watch and pray always,... ...lest ye be tempted by the devil, and ye be led away captive by him. 3 Nephi 18:15

And it came to pass that there was no contention in the land,... ...because of the love of God which did dwell in the hearts of the people. 4 Nephi 1:15

Adam fell that men might be;... ...and men are that they might have joy. 2 Nephi 2:25

For behold, this life is the time for men to prepare to meet God;... ...yea, behold the day of this life is the day for men to perform their labors. Alma 34:32

But charity is the pure love of Christ, and it endureth forever;... ...and whoso is found possessed of it at the last day, it shall be well with him. Moroni 7:47

For behold, I, God, have suffered these things for all, ...

...that they might not suffer if they would repent.

D&C 19:16

Be patient in afflictions for thou shalt have many; but endure them, ...

...for, lo, I am with thee, even unto the end of thy days.
D&C 24:8

Wherefore, be not weary in well-doing, for ye are laying the foundation of a great work.

And out of small things proceedeth that which is great.
D&C

Wherefore, be of good cheer, and do not fear, ...

...for I the Lord am with you, and will stand by you.

D&C 68:6

I, the Lord, am bound when ye do what I say; ...

...but when ye do not what I say, ye have no promise.
D&C 82:10

Therefore, care not for the body, neither the life of the body ...

...but care for the soul, and for the life of the soul.
D&C 101:37

He that findeth his life shall lose it;...

...and he that loseth his life for my sake shall find it. Matt. 10:39

For if ye forgive men their trespasses,...

...your heavenly Father will also forgive you. Matt. 6:14

Lay not up for yourselves treasures upon earth,...

...But lay up for yourselves treasures in heaven. Matt. 6:19-21

Choose you this day whom ye will serve;...

...but as for me and my house, we will serve the Lord. Joshua 24:15

If ye love me,...

...Keep my commandments. John 14:15

This is my work and my glory—...

...to bring to pass the immortality and eternal life of man. Moses 1:39

Repent & be baptized.

Stand ye in holy places.

Receive the truth.

Follow the Holy Spirit.

Do not be deceived.

My ♥ will not fail me. I will be prepared for Jesus' coming!

D&C 45:26

SERVICE: As I Serve I Learn Ways to Be Happy

(Service Station sack of reminders)

See lesson #39 in Primary 5 manual*.

YOU'LL NEED: Copy of sack label and service reminder wordstrips pattern (page 79), SCRIPTURE CHALLENGE CARD (page 110) on colored cardstock paper, small brown paper bag for each child, scissors, and crayons

ACTIVITY: (1) Color and cut out a Service Station label and glue on a brown paper bag. (2) Cut out service reminder wordstrips and place in bag. Encourage children to take this bag home and pull out acts of kindness each day/week to remind them to serve others. Talk about the rewards that come from service (e.g. making one feel happy, increasing talents, and the blessings that come from Heavenly Father). Encourage children to add to these deeds by making their own list of service.

*SCRIPTURE CHALLENGE**

THOUGHT TREAT: Lifesavers® Candy Cars. Give each child a whole pack of Lifesavers® candies (for the car body), and glue individual Lifesavers® on sides for the wheel.

Remind children that if they speed by others not stopping to serve, they could swerve off the straight and narrow path that leads back to our Heavenly Father.

TEMPLE MARRIAGE: I Will Live the Law of Chastity and Be Worthy

(temple light poster)

See lesson #44 in Primary 5 manual*.

YOU'LL NEED: Copy of temple light poster pattern (page 80), SCRIPTURE CHALLENGE CARD (page 112) on colored cardstock paper for each child, scissors, and crayons

ACTIVITY: Children can punch pin holes in this backwards picture. When they place it in the window (facing out) they can see the message written forward on the other side as the light shines through the pin hole dots.

*SCRIPTURE CHALLENGE**

THOUGHT TREAT: Temple Mints. Remind children that the law of chastity is sweet and will bring you closer to the temple to be married for this life and for eternity.

**SCRIPTURE CHALLENGE: Assign each child a new card and reward them with a glue-on sticker for the card completed.

PATTERN:
SERVICE (Service
Station sack
of reminders)

See lesson #39 in
Primary 5 manual*.

You're at the SERVICE STATION! Gas up, take off and help those you "car" about.

Read a story to sister or brother.	Rake leaves, but not in trees.
Make someone's bed.	Do Housework without a shirk.
Fix a snack, add a note, and deliver.	Fix breakfast for mom or dad.
Vacuum with vigor 10 minutes.	Ask your family how you can help.
Wipe mirrors with window cleaner.	Dust your best to pass the white glove test.
Set the table for invisible Aunt Mabel.	Pick out a recipe cook up a storm (great food)!
Visit and cheer up the elderly.	Make a vegetable snack for dinner.
Make a homemade gift and deliver.	Compliment someone by saying "cool ____," or "great ___."
Make, eat, and clean up after a snack.	Take a treat to someone on your street.
Be a dirt detective (sweep the floor).	Wash and wipe the dishes.

TEMPLES: I Will Live Worthy to Receive Temple Blessings

(child's photo in temple frame)   See lesson #35 in Primary 5 manual*.

YOU'LL NEED: Copy of temple frame pattern (page 83), SCRIPTURE CHALLENGE CARD (page 108) on colored cardstock paper for each child, scissors, crayons, and glue

ACTIVITY: Create a frame into which a child can insert his/her own photo next to the temple to remind them to live worthy of temple blessings. (1) Color and cut out temple frame (and inside area) and frame back.. (2) Ask child to place photo next to temple and glue frame sides to back of frame. Before, cut out flap in back piece and fold to stand up frame.

*SCRIPTURE CHALLENGE CARD***

THOUGHT TREAT: Temple Mints. Temple-shaped mints or other mints to tell children that Jesus Christ and Heavenly Father "mint" (meant) for all of us to share the blessings of the temple.

TESTIMONY: Study and Prayer Strengthen My Testimony

(TESTIMONY word race)   See lesson #46 in Primary 5 manual*.

YOU'LL NEED: Copy of TESTIMONY word design chart (page 83), SCRIPTURE CHALLENGE CARD (page 113) on colored cardstock paper for each child, pencils, and crayons

ACTIVITY: Race to find words that stem from the word TESTIMONY. (1) Divide class into two teams with their TESTIMONY word design chart in front of them. (2) With pencil in hand and two teams with chairs back to back, begin. (3) Use the letters in TESTIMONY to inspire other words that connect. Words can be written in any direction—left, right, up, down, or diagonal. (4) Once a word is written, other words can stem off the words written. All words must be words that are part of the gospel of Jesus Christ, words that help strengthen testimony. (5) Children can earn 10 points for every word that stems from the word TESTIMONY. (6) Children can earn 1 point for all words written after the first word that stems from the word TESTIMONY. See chart on this page if you run out ideas.

*SCRIPTURE CHALLENGE CARD***

THOUGHT TREAT: TESTIMONY Treats. Any food that begins with the letters in the word TESTIMONY, i.e.: taffy, egg, salt, toast, icing or ice cube, mustard, onion or orange, nut or noodle, yeast, yogurt, or yam. Activity #1: Place food items on a tray for children to see to play the memory game. Children can look at tray for 60 seconds (still divided into teams). Activity #2: Have children write the word TESTIMONY by placing treats in order, i.e., toast first and eggplant second. Be sure to share a treat with children, i.e., taffy, a dyed hard boiled egg (with letter "T"), or a small container of yogurt or yogurt covered raisins or peanuts.

**SCRIPTURE CHALLENGE: Assign each child a new card and reward them with a glue-on sticker for the card completed.

TESTIMONY WORD RACE!

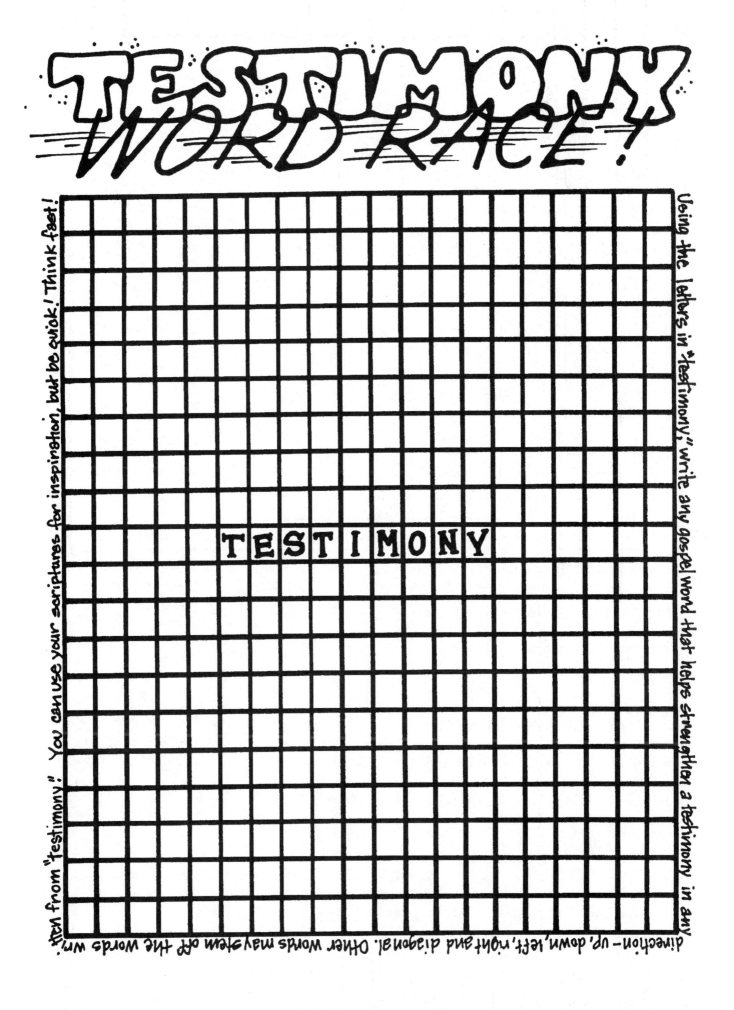

T E S T I M O N Y

Using the letters in "testimony," write any gospel word that helps strengthen a testimony in any direction—up, down, left, right and diagonal. Other words may stem off the words written from "testimony." You can use your scriptures for inspiration, but be quick! Think fast!

TITHING: I Will Pay a Full Tithing to Build Up the Kingdom of God

(origami tithing purse/wallet)

See lesson #45 in Primary 5 manual*.

YOU'LL NEED: Copy of origami tithing purse/wallet pattern (page 85), SCRIPTURE CHALLENGE CARD (page 113) on colored cardstock paper for each child, scissors, and crayons

ACTIVITY: Fold a tithing purse/wallet to hold tithing donations until child has the opportunity to pay. This purse/wallet can be placed in their scriptures for safekeeping. Remind children that each time they open this envelope to put money in to keep for tithing or take the money out to pay tithing, they receive a blessing from heaven.

1. Color and cut out purse/wallet pattern.
2. Follow steps #A-G to fold purse/wallet.

SCRIPTURE CHALLENGE*

THOUGHT TREAT: OPTION #1: 1/10th Cupcake. Bake a cupcake for each child and one for the bishop. Give each child 10 M&M pieces of candy. Each child places one candy on the bishop's cupcake and nine on their cupcake. Deliver cupcake with donations to the bishop.
OPTION #2: Tithing Store House Cake. Bake and frost a cake. With different colored frosting tubes, decorate cake with a tithing store house with goods a farmer might have brought as tithing payment. Example: Nine chicken eggs (or jelly beans) to the side for the farmer and one egg (or jelly bean) in the store house.

TRIALS STRENGTHEN: My Faith Grows as I Obey

(Premortal Life/Earth Life quiz)

See lesson #28 in Primary 5 manual*.

YOU'LL NEED: Copy of quiz pattern (page 86), SCRIPTURE CHALLENGE CARD (page 104) on colored cardstock paper for each child, and crayons

ACTIVITY: Tell children that their faith grows as they make right choices. Let's think about the choice we made to come to earth and write it in the Pre-Existence circle. Then, think about the choices you make on earth to pass the test, to go back to your heavenly home. OPTION: Use as a teaching tool. Children can cut out circles and arrow and children to show the bodies moving from pre-existence to earth life. FUN IDEA: Cut out a plastic doll using paper doll pattern (cut head on fold line). Plastic spirit should have two sides to slip over paper doll when showing how spirit enters and leaves the body.

SCRIPTURE CHALLENGE*

THOUGHT TREAT: Rope Licorice. Give each child a licorice rope (pull and peel style with 6 or more strands in each). Tell children that with each commandment they keep, that one commandment builds strength and helps you to keep the other commandments, just like each strand in this rope builds wraps around and strengthens the others.

**SCRIPTURE CHALLENGE: Assign each child a new card and reward them with a glue-on sticker for the card completed.

A. - Fold in half with illustrations on the outside.
B. - Fold corner over about two-thirds
C. - Fold opposite corner over and tuck in folds
D. - Fold the bottom edge up to meet the other corners
E. - Fold the top triangles down to new edge.
F. - To close wallet, tuck top triangle flap into fold.
G. - To find hidden pocket, separate top triangle corners.

VALIANT: I Will Live Valiantly the Gospel of Jesus Christ

(Valiant poster)

See lesson #43 in Primary 5 manual*.

YOU'LL NEED: Copy of Valiant poster pattern (page 88), SCRIPTURE CHALLENGE CARD (page 112) on colored cardstock paper for each child, and crayons

ACTIVITY: Encourage children to color and post on their wall this poster that asks them to live the gospel of Jesus Christ valiantly. Remind children of the words that describe the valiant pioneers and us today as we keep the commandments and endure to the end (*courageous, obedient, loving, kind, loyal, strong, true, faithful, honest, unselfish, patient, righteous, and forgiving*).

*SCRIPTURE CHALLENGE CARD***

THOUGHT TREAT: Option #1 Valiant Vegetables. Give each child a few fresh, raw vegetables, (carrots, celery, broccoli, etc). Provide a ranch dressing to dip them in. As you munch, talk about the valiant pioneers who planted crops for those who would follow. They had the pioneer spirit, of leaving behind something of value. Ask children what they would like to leave behind to prove that they are valiant.
Option #2 Faithful Fruit. Give children pieces of fresh fruit or dried fruit or fruit leather. Tell children that fruit trees took longer to grow but provided a longterm nourishment for pioneers as the fruit came up every year without replanting.

WORD OF WISDOM: I Will Say "No" to Harmful and "Yes" to Healthful

(Word of Wisdom voting ballot)

See lesson #24 in Primary 5 manual*.

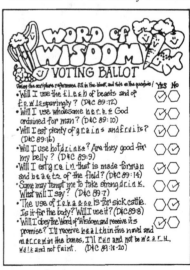

YOU'LL NEED: Copy of Word of Wisdom voting ballot pattern (page 89), SCRIPTURE CHALLENGE CARD (page 102) on colored cardstock paper, and a punch tack (to punch ballot) for each child, scissors, glue, and crayons

ACTIVITY: Help children vote "No" to harmful things for the body and "Yes" to healthful things. This voting process helps children decide to keep the Word of Wisdom revelation found in Doctrine and Covenants sections 88-89. (1) Color and cut out voting ballot. (2) Children read statement and vote "yes" or "no" by punching the column next to the statement. (3) Children can look up the scriptures and fill in the blank as they read the statements next to the scripture references.

*SCRIPTURE CHALLENGE CARD***

THOUGHT TREAT: Healthful Choice Food. Provide several healthful foods (e.g., raw fruit and vegetables) for children to choose from. Talk about the variety of foods we have to choose from that are healthful. Be sure to bless the food and thank Heavenly Father for the healthful choices we have and for the revelation of the Word of Wisdom given to us through the Prophet Joseph Smith.

**SCRIPTURE CHALLENGE: Assign each child a new card and reward them with a glue-on sticker for the card completed.

*Primary 5 manual is published by The Church of Jesus Christ of Latter-day Saints, Salt Lake City, Utah.

87

I will live **VALIENTLY** the gospel of Jesus Christ.

WORD of WISDOM
VOTING BALLOT

Using the scripture references, fill in the blank and vote on the questions!

	YES	NO

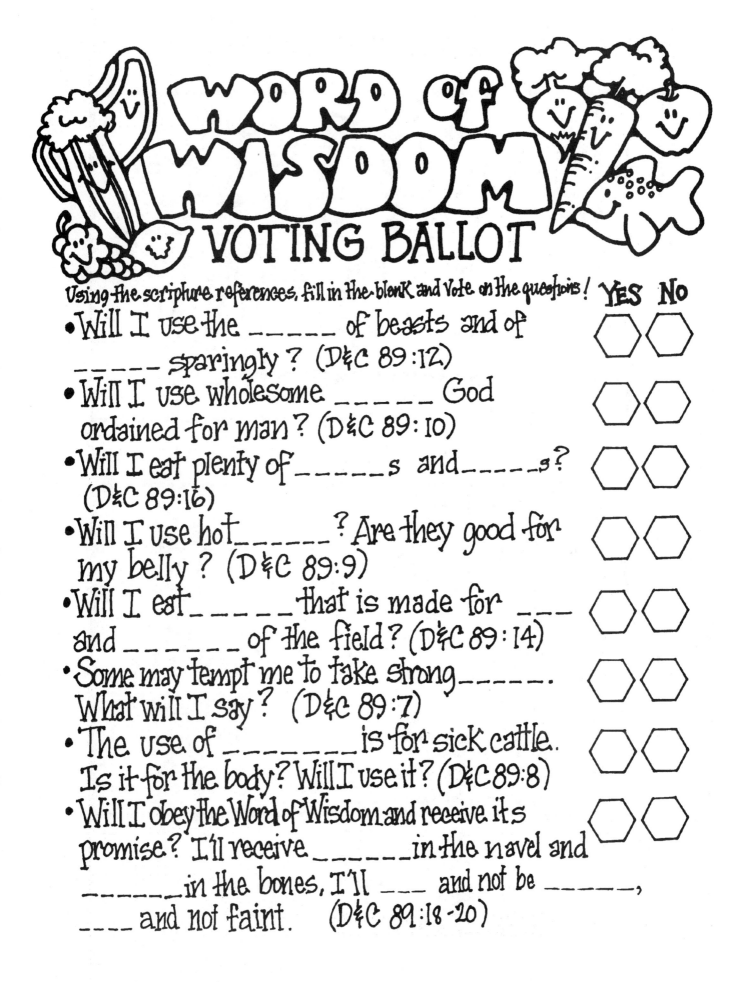

• Will I use the _____ of beasts and of _____ sparingly? (D&C 89:12)

• Will I use wholesome _____ God ordained for man? (D&C 89:10)

• Will I eat plenty of _____ s and _____ s? (D&C 89:16)

• Will I use hot _____? Are they good for my belly? (D&C 89:9)

• Will I eat _____ that is made for ___ and _____ of the field? (D&C 89:14)

• Some may tempt me to take strong _____. What will I say? (D&C 89:7)

• The use of _____ is for sick cattle. Is it for the body? Will I use it? (D&C 89:8)

• Will I obey the Word of Wisdom and receive its promise? I'll receive _____ in the navel and _____ in the bones, I'll ___ and not be _____, ___ and not faint. (D&C 89:18-20)

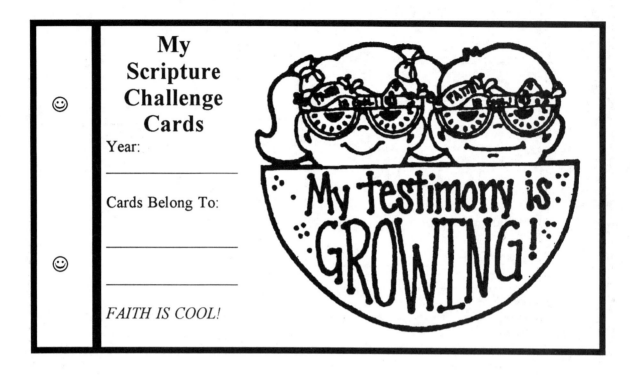

My Scripture Challenge Cards

Year:

_____

Cards Belong To:

_____

_____

FAITH IS COOL!

SCRIPTURE CHALLENGE
How to Use Cards to Help Your Testimony Grow:

SEARCH & PONDER CHALLENGE:

1. Read the scriptures assigned on the cards each week to build your testimony.
2. Fill in missing words on featured scripture.
3. Reward yourself for scriptures read.
   COLOR, CUT OUT, AND GLUE LARGE PICTURE OVER SMALL PICTURE IN CARDS #1-46 TO SHOW THAT YOUR TESTIMONY IS GROWING.
4. Post the scripture card on mirror to memorize.
5. Collect and laminate cards #1-46.
6. Learn and try the Book of Mormon promise in Moroni 10:4-5 (to know the truth of all things).

FIRST VISION: #1
Joseph Smith Saw Heavenly Father and Jesus

SEARCH & PONDER CHALLENGE:
Read This Week:
Joseph Smith—History 1:1-20

Joseph Smith—History 1:18-19 "No sooner, therefore, did I get possession of myself, so as to be able to speak, than I asked the Personages who __ __ __ __ __ above me in the light, which of all the sects was __ __ __ __ __ (for ... it had never entered into my heart that __ __ __ were wrong)--and which I should join. I was answered that I must join __ __ __ __ of them."

APOSTASY: #2
Jesus Christ's Church Is Restored

SEARCH & PONDER CHALLENGE:
Read This Week: D&C 1:17-23

D&C 1:17-18, 21, 23

"I the Lord ... called ... upon my servant Joseph Smith, Jun., and spake unto him from heaven, and gave him commandments; And also gave commandments to others that they should proclaim ... unto the world; ... That __ __ __ __ __ also might increase in the earth; ... That the fulness of my __ __ __ __ __ __ __ might be proclaimed.

GOSPEL FULNESS:
Angel Moroni's Good News Message

#3

SEARCH & PONDER CHALLENGE:
Read This Week:
Joseph Smith—History 1:30-35

Joseph Smith—History 1:34-35 "He said there was a __ __ __ __ deposited, written upon __ __ __ __ __ __ __ __ __ __, giving an account of the former inhabitants of this continent, ... that the fulness of the everlasting __ __ __ __ __ __ was contained in it, as delivered by the Savior to the ancient inhabitants ... Also ... the __ __ __ __ and Thummim [was] deposited with the plates."

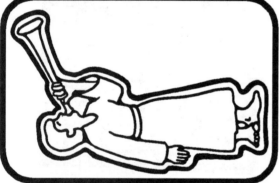

PREPARE:
I Will Prepare to Serve Jesus and Others

#4

SEARCH & PONDER CHALLENGE:
Read This Week:
Joseph Smith—History 1:53-58

Joseph Smith—History 1:55 "As my father's worldly circumstances were very limited, we were under the necessity of __ __ __ __ __ __ __ __ __ with our hands, hiring out by day's __ __ __ __ and otherwise, as we could get opportunity ... and by continuous __ __ __ __ __ were enabled to get a comfortable maintenance."

OBEDIENCE: #5
Heavenly Father Will Help Me As I Obey

SEARCH & PONDER CHALLENGE:
Read: Joseph Smith—History 1:59-60

Joseph Smith—History 1:59-60 "At length the time arrived for obtaining the plates ... (write month, day, and year here

_ _ _ _ _ _ _ _ _ _, _ _,

_ _ _ _).... The same heavenly messenger

_ _ _ _ _ _ _ _ _ _ them up to me

with this charge: that I should be

_ _ _ _ _ _ _ _ _ _ _ _ for them;

... [and] preserve them, until he, the

messenger, should call for them."

PRAYER: #6
I Will Seek Heavenly Father's Guidance

SEARCH & PONDER CHALLENGE:
Read This Week:
D&C 3:1-3 and 10:1-5

D&C 3:2
"For God doth not walk in

_ _ _ _ _ _ _ _ paths, neither doth he

turn to the right hand nor to the left, neither

doth he vary from that which he hath said,

therefore his _ _ _ _ _ _ are

_ _ _ _ _ _ _ _ _, and his course is

one _ _ _ _ _ _ _ _ round."

HOLY GHOST: #7
The Holy Ghost Will Guide and Comfort Me

SEARCH & PONDER CHALLENGE:
Read This Week: D&C 8:2-3

D&C 8:2-3
"Yea, behold, I will tell you in your
__ __ __ __ and in your __ __ __ __ __ , by
the Holy Ghost, which shall come upon you
and which shall dwell in your heart. Now,
behold, this is the __ __ __ __ __ __ of
revelation; behold, this is the spirit by which
__ __ __ __ __ brought the children of Israel
through the __ __ __ Sea on dry ground."

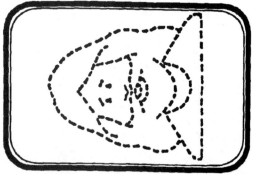

PRIESTHOOD BLESSINGS: #8
I Will Be Worthy to Receive Blessings

SEARCH & PONDER CHALLENGE:
Read This Week: D&C 13 (and heading)

D&C 13
"Upon you my fellow servants, in the name of
Messiah I confer the
__ __ __ __ __ __ __ __ __ __ __ of Aaron,
which holds the keys of the ministering of
__ __ __ __ __ __ , and of the gospel of
repentance, and of baptism by immersion for
the remission of sins."

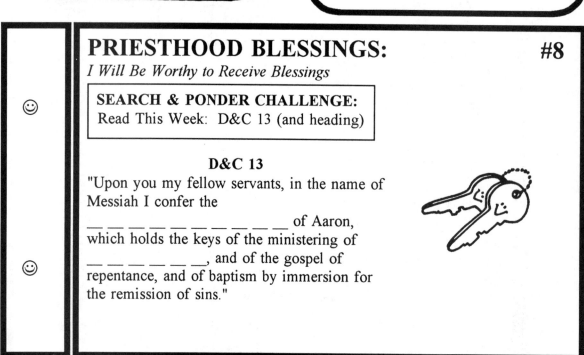

BOOK OF MORMON: #9
I Will Bear My Testimony of Truth

> **SEARCH & PONDER CHALLENGE:**
> Read This Week: D&C 17:1-4

D&C 17:1, 3
"You shall have a __ __ __ __ of the plates ...
and also the breastplate, the sword of Laban,
the Urim and __ __ __ __ __ __ __ which
were given to the brother of
__ __ __ __ __ upon the mount, when he
talked with the Lord face to face, and the
miraculous directors which were given to
__ __ __ __ ... And ... you shall testify of
them by the power of __ __ __."

BOOK OF MORMON PUBLICATION: #10
I'm Grateful I Have It to Read and Study

> **SEARCH & PONDER CHALLENGE:**
> Read This Week: D&C 20:8-12
> and Introduction of Book of Mormon

D&C 20:8-9, 11-12
"God ... gave him [Joseph Smith] power ... to
__ __ __ __ __ __ __ __ __ the Book of
Mormon; Which contains a record of a fallen
people, and the fulness of the gospel of Jesus
Christ ... Proving ... the holy scriptures are
__ __ __ __, ... showing that he is the same
God yesterday, today, and
__ __ __ __ __ __ __."

RESTORATION: #11
The True Church Was Restored to the Earth

SEARCH & PONDER CHALLENGE:
Read Week: D&C 20:1-4 and 21:1-5

D&C 115:4

"For thus shall my __ __ __ __ __ __ be

called in the last days, even The Church of

__ __ __ __ __   __ __ __ __ __ __ of

__ __ __ __ __ __ -day __ __ __ __ __ __.

ORDINANCES RESTORED: #12
I'm Grateful to Be Baptized

SEARCH & PONDER CHALLENGE:
Read This Week: D&C 20:72-79
and 2 Nephi 31:17-21

D&C 20:37
"All those who __ __ __ __ __ __ __ themselves
before God, and desire to be baptized, and
come forth with __ __ __ __ __ __ hearts and
__ __ __ __ __ __ __ __ __ spirits, and ... have
truly repented of all their sins, and are willing
to take upon them the __ __ __ __ of Jesus
Christ, ... to __ __ __ __ __ him to the end ...
shall be received by baptism into his church."

MISSIONARY: #13
I Will Share The Gospel of Jesus Christ

SEARCH & PONDER CHALLENGE:
Read This Week: D&C, Section 4

D&C 4:2

"Therefore, O ye that embark in the
__ __ __ __ __ __ __ of God, see that ye
__ __ __ __ __ __ him with all your
__ __ __ __ __ __, might, __ __ __ __ and
__ __ __ __ __ __ __ __ __, that ye may stand
blameless before God at the __ __ __ __
day."

Serve a Mission

HYMNS: #14
The Sacred Hymns Bring Us Blessings

SEARCH & PONDER CHALLENGE:
Read This Week: D&C, Section 25

D&C 25:12

"For my __ __ __ __ delighteth in the
__ __ __ __ __ of the __ __ __ __ __; yea, the
song of the righteous is a __ __ __ __ __ __
unto me, and it shall be answered with a
__ __ __ __ __ __ __ __ __ upon their heads."

REVELATION: #15
The Prophet Speaks and I Listen

SEARCH & PONDER CHALLENGE:
Read This Week: D&C 43:1-7

D&C 43:7

"For verily I say unto you, that he that is
__ __ __ __ __ __ __ __ of me shall come in
at the __ __ __ __ and be ordained as I have
told you before, to __ __ __ __ __ those
revelations which you have received and shall
receive through him whom I have
__ __ __ __ __ __ __ __."

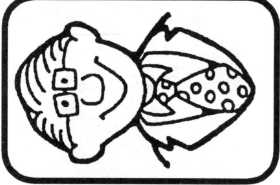

LOVE AND UNITY: #16
I Will Love and Help Others

SEARCH & PONDER CHALLENGE:
Read This Week: D&C 38:24, 31-32

D&C 38:24

"And let every man __ __ __ __ __ __ his
brother as __ __ __ __ __ __ __ __, and practise
__ __ __ __ __ __ __ and holiness before me."

Love Others

BISHOPS: #17
I Will Support My Church Leaders

SEARCH & PONDER CHALLENGE:
Read This Week: D&C 41:9-11

D&C 41:9, 11

"I have called my servant Edward Partridge; and I give a commandment, that he should be appointed by the voice of the church, and
___ ___ ___ ___ ___ ___ ___ a ___ ___ ___ ___ ___
unto the church ... And this because his
___ ___ ___ ___ ___ is ___ ___ ___ ___ before me ..."

LAW OF CONSECRATION: #18
I Will Share to Build Up the Kingdom of God

SEARCH & PONDER CHALLENGE:
Read This Week: D&C 42:34-39

D&C 42:38

"For inasmuch as ye ___ ___ it unto the
___ ___ ___ ___ ___ of these, ye ___ ___ it
unto me."

GIFTS OF THE SPIRIT: #19
I Can Recognize and Seek True Gifts

SEARCH & PONDER CHALLENGE:
Read This Week: D&C 46:11-14, 17-26

D&C 46:11, 14
"For all have not every __ __ __ __ given unto them; for there are many gifts, and to __ __ __ __ __ __ man is given a gift by the __ __ __ __ __ __ __ of God."
<u>Gift of a Testimony</u>:
"To others it is given to believe on their words, that they also might have eternal life if they continue __ __ __ __ __ __ __ __."

SCRIPTURES: #20
I Love to Study the Scriptures

SEARCH & PONDER CHALLENGE:
Read second half of Introductory Note for the Pearl of Great Price (explains content)

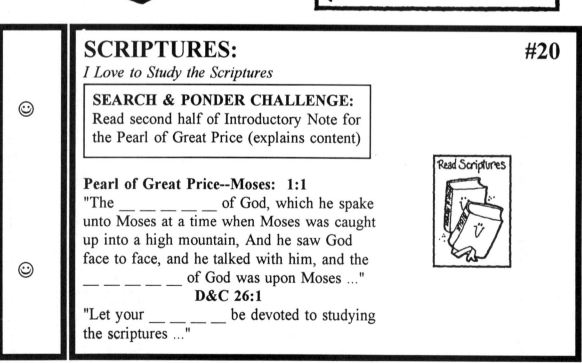

Pearl of Great Price--Moses: 1:1
"The __ __ __ __ __ of God, which he spake unto Moses at a time when Moses was caught up into a high mountain, And he saw God face to face, and he talked with him, and the __ __ __ __ __ of God was upon Moses ..."

D&C 26:1
"Let your __ __ __ __ be devoted to studying the scriptures ..."

FORGIVENESS: #21
I Will Forgive Others and Find Peace

SEARCH & PONDER CHALLENGE:
Read This Week: D&C 64:9-11

D&C 64:9-10

"Ye ought to __ __ __ __ __ __ __ one
another; for he that forgiveth __ __ __ his
brother his __ __ __ __ __ __ __ __ __ __
standeth condemned before the Lord; for there
remaineth in him the __ __ __ __ __ __ __ __
sin. I, the Lord, will __ __ __ __ __ __ __ __
whom I will forgive, but of you it is required
to forgive __ __ __ men."

REVELATION: #22
The Prophets Give Latter-day Revelation

SEARCH & PONDER CHALLENGE:
Read This Week: D&C 67:4

D&C 67:4

"And now I, the Lord, give unto you a
__ __ __ __ __ __ __ __ __ __ __ of the
__ __ __ __ __ __ of these
__ __ __ __ __ __ __ __ __ __ __ __ which
are lying before you."

CELESTIAL KINGDOM: #23
I Can to Live With Heavenly Father Again

SEARCH & PONDER CHALLENGE:
Read This Week: D&C 76:11-24

D&C 76:22-23
"And now, after the many testimonies which have been given of him, this is the testimony, last of all, which we give of him: That he __ __ __ __ __ __! For we __ __ __ him, even on the right hand of __ __ __; and we heard the voice bearing record that he is the Only Begotten of the Father."

WORD OF WISDOM: #24
I Will Say "No" to Harmful/"Yes" to Healthful

SEARCH & PONDER CHALLENGE:
Read This Week: D&C 89:4-14, 18-21

D&C 89:18-21
"And all saints who remember to keep and do these sayings, walking in obedience to the commandments, shall receive __ __ __ __ __ __ __ in their navel and marrow to their __ __ __ __ __ __; And shall find wisdom and great treasures of knowledge, even __ __ __ __ __ __ __ treasures; And shall run and not be weary, and shall walk and not faint."

SACRIFICE: #25

Heavenly Father Blesses Me When I Sacrifice

> **SEARCH & PONDER CHALLENGE:**
> Read: D&C 88:119 and 95:11-12

D&C 88:119-120

"__ __ __ __ __ __ __ __ yourselves; prepare
every needful thing; and establish a house,
even a house of prayer, a house of fasting, a
house of faith, a house of learning, a house of
glory, a house of order, a house of God; That
your incomings may be in the name of the
Lord; that your __ __ __ __ __ __ __ __ __
may be in the name of the Lord ..."

PRIESTHOOD KEYS   #26

Help Us Do Missionary and Temple Work

> **SEARCH & PONDER CHALLENGE:**
> Read This Week: D&C 110

D&C 110:11 Keys to Do Missionary Work:
"Moses appeared before us, and committed unto
us the keys of the
__ __ __ __ __ __ __ __ __ of Israel from the
four parts of the earth ..."

**D&C 110:13-16 Keys of Sealing Power--
Temple Work:** "Elijah the prophet ... [was] ...
sent, to turn the __ __ __ __ __ __ of the
fathers to the children, and the children to the
fathers."

COMMANDMENTS:

#27

I Will Be Blessed as I Obey and Endure

SEARCH & PONDER CHALLENGE:
Read This Week: D&C 82:10

D&C 82:10

"I, the Lord, am __ __ __ __ __ when ye __ __ what I say; but when ye do not what I say, ye have no __ __ __ __ __ __ __ __."

TRIALS STRENGTHEN:

#28

My Faith Grows As I Obey

SEARCH & PONDER CHALLENGE:
Read This Week: D&C 105:1-6, 9-10

D&C 105:6

"And my people must needs be chastened until they learn __ __ __ __ __ __ __ __ __ __, if it must needs be, by the things which they __ __ __ __ __ __."

MISSIONARY: #29
I Will Share the Gospel of Jesus Christ

> **SEARCH & PONDER CHALLENGE:**
> Read: D&C 107:23 and 112:10, 19

D&C 112:10, 19

"Be thou __ __ __ __ __ __; and the Lord thy
God shall lead thee by the hand, and give thee
answer to thy prayers. ... Wherefore,
whithersoever they shall send you, go ye, and
I will be with you; and in whatsoever place
ye shall __ __ __ __ __ __ __ __ my name
an effectual door shall be __ __ __ __ __ __
unto you, that they may receive my word."

SECOND COMING: #30
I Will Prepare to Meet My Savior Jesus Christ

> **SEARCH & PONDER CHALLENGE:**
> Read: D&C 29:10-11 and 107:53-56

D&C 29:10-11

"For the __ __ __ __ is nigh, and that which
was spoken by mine apostles must be fulfilled;
for as they spoke so shall it come to pass; For
I will __ __ __ __ __ __ myself from heaven
with power and great glory, with all the hosts
thereof, and dwell in righteousness with men
on earth a thousand years, and the wicked shall
__ __ __ stand."

PROPHET GUIDES: #31
I Will Listen to the Prophet and Obey

> **SEARCH & PONDER CHALLENGE:**
> Read This Week: D&C 105:6-10

D&C 105:10
"That they themselves may be
_ _ _ _ _ _ _ _ _, and that my people
may be _ _ _ _ _ _ _ more perfectly,
and have _ _ _ _ _ _ _ _ _ _ _, and
_ _ _ _ more perfectly concerning their
_ _ _ _, and the things which I require at
their hands."

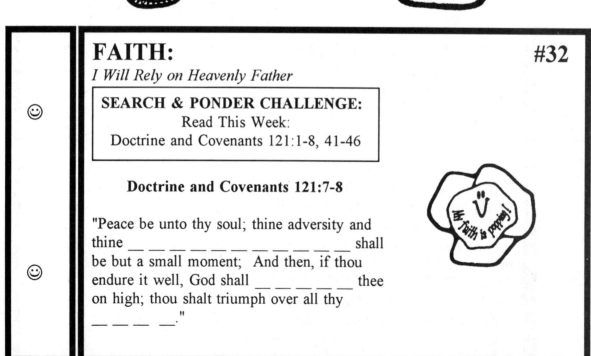

FAITH: #32
I Will Rely on Heavenly Father

> **SEARCH & PONDER CHALLENGE:**
> Read This Week:
> Doctrine and Covenants 121:1-8, 41-46

Doctrine and Covenants 121:7-8

"Peace be unto thy soul; thine adversity and
thine _ _ _ _ _ _ _ _ _ _ _ _ _ shall
be but a small moment; And then, if thou
endure it well, God shall _ _ _ _ _ thee
on high; thou shalt triumph over all thy
_ _ _ _."

PIONEER SPIRIT: #33
I Will Work Hard to Leave a Legacy of Love

SEARCH & PONDER CHALLENGE:
Read This Week:
D&C 58:27-28 and 88:124

D&C 88:27-28
"Verily I say, men should be anxiously
__ __ __ __ __ __ __ in a good cause, and do
many things of their own free __ __ __ __,
and bring to pass much righteousness;
For the __ __ __ __ __ is in them, wherein
they are agents unto themselves. And
inasmuch as men do __ __ __ __ they shall in
nowise lose their __ __ __ __ __ __."

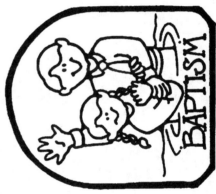

BAPTISM FOR THE DEAD: #34
Others Who Have Died Can Be Baptized

SEARCH & PONDER CHALLENGE:
Read: John 3:5, D&C 128:15; 138:29-34

D&C 128:15
"These are principles in relation to the dead and
the living that cannot be lightly passed over, as
pertaining to our __ __ __ __ __ __ __ __ __ __.
For their salvation is necessary and essential to
our salvation, as Paul says concerning the
fathers—that they without us __ __ __ __ __ __
be made __ __ __ __ __ __ __—neither can we
without our dead be made perfect."

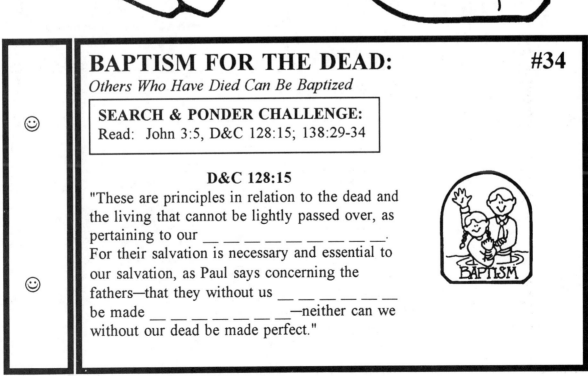

TEMPLES: #35
I Will Live Worthy to Receive Blessings

SEARCH & PONDER CHALLENGE:
Read: D&C 124:26-29, 40-45

D&C 124:40-41

"And verily I say unto you, let this house be built unto my name that I may reveal mine __ __ __ __ __ __ __ __ __ __ __ therein unto my people. For I deign to reveal unto my church things which have been kept __ __ __ from before the foundation of the world, things that pertain to the dispensation of the fulness of times."

ARTICLES OF FAITH   #36
Strengthen My Testimony

SEARCH & PONDER CHALLENGE:
Articles of Faith in Pearl of Great Price

Articles of Faith 1:13 "We believe in being __ __ __ __ __ __, true, chaste, benevolent, virtuous, and in doing good to all men; indeed, we may say that we __ __ __ __ __ __ __ the admonition of Paul—We believe all things, we hope all things, we have endured many things, and __ __ __ __ to be able to __ __ __ __ __ __ all things. If there is anything virtuous, lovely, or of __ __ __ __ report or praiseworthy, we __ __ __ __ after these things."

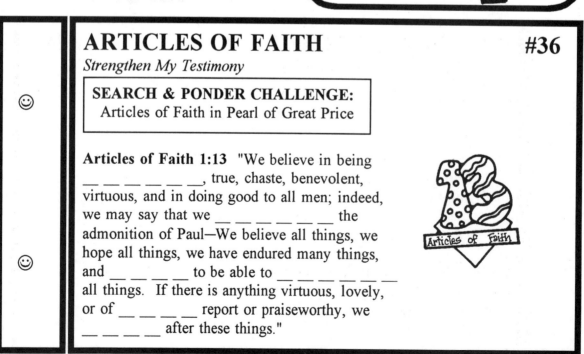

PROPHET JOSEPH SMITH   #37
Restored the Gospel of Jesus Christ

SEARCH & PONDER CHALLENGE:
Read This Week: D&C 135:1-4

D&C 135:3
"Joseph Smith, the _ _ _ _ _ _ _ _ and
_ _ _ _ of the Lord, has done more, save
Jesus only, for the <u>salvation</u> of men in this
world, than any other man that ever lived in
it. In the short space of twenty years, he has
brought forth the Book of Mormon, which he
_ _ _ _ _ _ _ _ _ _ by the
_ _ _ _ and power of God ..."

PROPHET OF TODAY   #38
Was Called By God to Lead Us

SEARCH & PONDER CHALLENGE:
This Week Read: D&C 112:30-32

D&C 112:30
"For unto you, the Twelve, and those, the First
_ _ _ _ _ _ _ _ _ _ _, who are
appointed with you to be your counselors and
your leaders, is the power of this
_ _ _ _ _ _ _ _ _ _ _ given, for the
last days and for the last time, in which is the
dispensation of the _ _ _ _ _ _ _ of
times."

SERVICE: #39
As I Serve I Learn Ways to Be Happy

SEARCH & PONDER CHALLENGE:
Read This Week: Mosiah 2:17

Mosiah 2:17
"And behold, I tell you these things that ye
may learn _ _ _ _ _ _ _; that ye may
learn that when ye are in the
_ _ _ _ _ _ _ of your fellow beings
ye are only in the service of your God."

Alma 40:12
"The _ _ _ _ _ _ _ _ of those who are
righteous are received into a state of
_ _ _ _ _ _ _ _ _ _ ..."

GRATITUDE: #40
I Will Work Hard to Serve Like the Pioneers

SEARCH & PONDER CHALLENGE:
Read: D&C 136:1-5, 7, 28-29

D&C 136:2
"Let all the people of the Church of Jesus Christ
of Latter-day Saints, and those who journey with
them, be _ _ _ _ _ _ _ _ _ _ into
companies, with a covenant and promise to keep
all the _ _ _ _ _ _ _ _ _ _ _ _ _ _,
with a covenant and promise to _ _ _ _
all the commandments and statutes of the Lord
our God."

SABBATH DAY: #41
I Will Keep the Sabbath Day Holy

> **SEARCH & PONDER CHALLENGE:**
> Read: D&C 59:7-19 and 78:19

D&C 59:9-10

"And that thou mayest more fully keep thyself unspotted from the world, thou shalt go to the house of prayer and __ __ __ __ __ __ up thy sacraments upon my __ __ __ __ day;
For verily this is a day appointed unto you to __ __ __ __ from your labors, and to __ __ __ thy devotions unto the Most High."

FAITH: #42
Faith in Jesus Christ Helps with Problems

> **SEARCH & PONDER CHALLENGE:**
> Read This Week: D&C 8:10 and 20:29

D&C 10:52, 55, 57-58 "And now, behold, according to their __ __ __ __ __ in their prayers will I bring this part of my gospel to the knowledge of my people. Behold, I do not bring it to destroy that which they have received, but to build it up. ... Therefore, whosoever belongeth to my church need not __ __ __ __, for such shall inherit the kingdom of heaven. ... I am Jesus Christ, ... the light which shineth in darkness ..."

VALIANT: #43

Live Valiantly the Gospel of Jesus Christ

SEARCH & PONDER CHALLENGE:
Read This Week: D&C 14:7 and 24:8

D&C 14:7

"And, if you _ _ _ _ my commandments
and _ _ _ _ _ _ to the end you shall
have eternal _ _ _ _, which gift is the
greatest of all the gifts of _ _ _."

TEMPLE MARRIAGE: #44

I Will Live the Law of Chastity and Be Worthy

SEARCH & PONDER CHALLENGE:
Read: D&C 131:1-4 & 132:15-21

D&C 131:1-4

"In the _ _ _ _ _ _ _ _ _ _ glory there
are three heavens or degrees; And in order to
obtain the highest, a man must enter into this
order of the priesthood [meaning the new and
everlasting covenant of

_ _ _ _ _ _ _ _ _]; And if he does not,
he cannot obtain it. He may enter into the
_ _ _ _ _, but that is the end of his
kingdom; he cannot have an increase."

TITHING: #45

Pay a Full Tithing to Build God's Kingdom

> **SEARCH & PONDER CHALLENGE:**
> Read This Week: Malachi 3:8-12 (Bible)

Malachi 3:10

"Bring ye all the __ __ __ __ __ __ into the storehouse, that there may be meat in mine house, and prove me now herewith, saith the Lord of hosts, if I will not open you the __ __ __ __ __ __ __ of heaven, and pour you out a blessing, that there shall not be room enough to receive it."

TESTIMONY: #46

Study and Prayer Strengthen My Testimony

> **SEARCH & PONDER CHALLENGE:**
> Read: Moroni 10:3-5 (The Book of Mormon Promise) D&C 1:30, 76:22-23

Moroni 10:4-5 "And when ye shall receive these things, ... __ __ __ God, the Eternal Father, in the name of Christ, if these things are not __ __ __ __; and if ye shall ask with a sincere heart, with __ __ __ __ intent, having faith in Christ, he will manifest the __ __ __ __ __ of it unto you, by the power of the Holy Ghost. And by the __ __ __ __ __ of the Holy Ghost ye may know the truth of all things"

Mary H. Ross, Author and
Jennette Guymon, Illustrator
are also the creators of:

PRIMARY PARTNERS:
A-Z Activities to Make Learning Fun for:

- Nursery and Age 3 (Sunbeams)
- CTR A & B Ages 4-7
- Book of Mormon Ages 8-11 (and more)
- Achievement Days, Girls Ages 8-11

MARY H. ROSS, Author

Mary Ross is an energetic mother, Primary teacher, and Achievement Days leader for two years, who loves to help children have a good time while they learn. She is a published author and columnist who has studied acting and taught modeling and voice. Her varied interests include writing, creating activities and children's parties, and cooking. Mary and her husband, Paul, live with their daughter, Jennifer in Sandy, Utah.

- Photos by Scott Hancock, Provo, Utah

JENNETTE GUYMON, Illustrator

Jennette Guymon has studied graphic arts and illustration at Utah Valley State College and the University of Utah. She is currently employed with a commercial construction company. She served a mission to Japan. Jennette enjoys sports, reading, cooking, art, and freelance illustrating. Jennette lives in Riverton, Utah.

More *PRIMARY PARTNERS*

Each activity is listed alphabetically and cross-referenced to a particular lesson in the Primary manuals. With appealing art work and fun-to-do games and crafts children will remember the message taught. Use these every week in Primary, of course ... but don't forget family home evening, where the good times get even better.

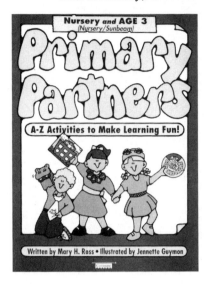

With this Nursery and Age 3 volume you can help a toddler appreciate the scriptures, and understand what it means to be reverent. You'll enjoy the 46 fun and unique crafts and activities contained in this book. Even the youngest children can learn important gospel principles.

As the Primary lesson subjects for ages 8-11 coordinate with the adult scriptures taught, both child and parent can enjoy reading the scriptures together year-after-year. For example, this *Primary Partners* activities match with the Book of Mormon lessons in the Primary 4 manual.

Children this age enjoy challenges to help them develop faith in Jesus Christ, put on the armor of God, keep baptismal covenants, and be a good example, like the heroes found in the Book of Mormon.

For example, this temple tie and tithing purse is send home as a reminder that families can be forever.

Some Activities Are:
♥ Example sandals to follow Jesus
♥ I Have "Bean" Obedient bean bag
♥ Bird watch and bug jar
♥ Family face block
♥ Reverent mouse maze
♥ Family prayer fan
♥ Fish Bowl, fish and pole
♥ Smile and frown flip-flag
♥ Animals Help Me sticker fun
♥ 3-D Noah's ark

To help children ages 4-7 Choose The Right, enjoy using these Primary 2-CTR A or Primary 3-CTR B volume to send them home with fun visuals: A pair of resurrection glasses to make the statement, "All eyes can see again!" Or, they can wear a band-aid bandelo to show that "When it is sick that I am feeling, I'll let the priesthood do the healing." These growing spirits can learn about tithing, service, forgiveness, reverence and ... MORE:
♥ Heavenly Family Photo
♥ Choices situation slap game
♥ Ammon "script"ure scene
♥ Forgiving Faces
♥ CTR happiness wheel (above)
♥ Prayer rock poem
♥ Dare to Be True wristbands
♥ Gratitude Gopher grab bag
♥ Scripture scroll
♥ Wise and foolish man flip-flag

Some Testimony Builders Are:
♥ Fight for Right! word choice
♥ 3-D box with Tree of Life Vision
♥ Nephite & Lamanite peace poster
♥ Waters of Mormon word search

Here's another fun-filled, information-packed book focusing on each of the Achievement Days goals. Leaders, you will never be at a loss when it comes to choosing activities or projects to make goal achievement memorable.

You can make these activities simple or elaborate. Whatever your choice, you'll all be in for a great time! Start each activity with an invitation to create interest, for a year's worth of "go"al get 'em activities!

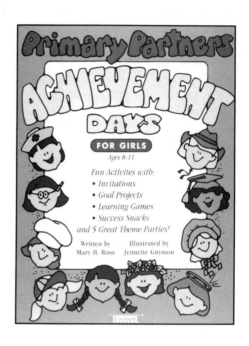

YOU'LL FIND:

MOTIVATIONAL PARTIES

Pop Into the Future!
Soar to Success!
Dad and Me Western Jamboree
Mom and Miss Pig-nic
Burstin' with Pride!

GOAL ACTIVITIES

ARTS & CRAFTS
Let's Make Pop-ups!
You're On Stage!

EDUCATION & SCHOLARSHIP
Wishin' in the Wishin' Well
Be a Jelly Bean Reader

FAMILY HISTORY
My Family Tree and Me
Journal Jazz!

FAMILY SKILLS
I Can Cook!
Super Sitter Basics

HEALTH & PERSONAL GROOMING
An Apple-a-Day the Healthy Way
Closet Class!

SPIRITUALITY
B.E.A.R.S.
(Be Enthusiastic About Reading Scriptures)
Home Sweet Home

OUTDOOR FUN & SKILLS
Ladybug Gardening Fun!
Nature Photo-rama!

PERSONAL PREPAREDNESS
I Can Eat an Elephant!
My Cents-able Savings Plan

SAFETY & EMERGENCY PREPAREDNESS
I Can Be Safe
First Aid Station

SERVICE & CITIZENSHIP
Hop to it! Service
That Grand Old Flag!

HOSPITALITY
Friends Forever!
Let's Be Pen Pals!

SPORTS & PHYSICAL FITNESS
Three Cheers for Good Sport!
Freta Frog's Fitness Fun